# HANNIBAL
## AN AFRICAN HERO

# HANNIBAL
## AN AFRICAN HERO

William J. Jacobs

Content Consultant:
Professor Richard F. W. Whittemore,
Teachers College, Columbia University

McGraw-Hill Book Company
New York    St. Louis    San Francisco    Düsseldorf
Johannesburg    Kuala Lumpur    London    Mexico
Montreal    New Delhi    Panama    Rio de Janeiro
Singapore    Sydney    Toronto

For Cathy and Adam

Library of Congress Cataloging in Publication Data

Jacobs, William Jay.
    Hannibal, an African hero.

    SUMMARY: A biography of Hannibal whose military
tactics baffled the Roman Empire's finest generals and
whose campaigns are still studied with interest by mili-
tary strategists.
    1. Hannibal—Juvenile literature. [1. Hannibal. 2.
Military biography. 3. Punic War, 2d, 218–201 B.C.]
I. Title.
DG249.3.J3    937'.04'0924   [B]   [92]    72–13165
ISBN 0–07–032157–4

# TABLE OF
# CONTENTS

# FOREWORD

"Hannibal's at the gates! Hannibal's at the gates!" Crowds of men and women hurried fearfully toward the Forum for the latest news. In generations to come Roman mothers would sometimes threaten their disobedient children, "Hannibal will get you if you aren't good." But on that tense afternoon in the year 216 B.C. the name Hannibal was no laughing matter to the panic-stricken citizens of mighty Rome.

The daring Carthaginian leader was poised with his powerful army within sight of the city's walls. Would he strike? Would he offer a humiliating peace? Outnumbered as always since he stormed over the impassable Alps with his fearful war elephants, could Hannibal again outwit the vaunted Roman legions? Would he slash them to bloody ribbons as he had at Cannae? Was Rome to be bludgeoned to her knees?

For a brief moment in time the fate of the entire Mediterranean world hung suspended, breathlessly awaiting the will of one man—Hannibal.

Who was Hannibal? What kind of man was he? What passion drove him to devote his entire lifetime to one task—the destruction of Rome?

Strangely, for all his importance in history, the figure of Hannibal remains shrouded in mystery. No known coin bears his profile; no statue to him survives. All has vanished except for the saga of his military triumphs. And even the record of his campaigns has been preserved for us mainly by the historians of Rome, the dread enemy of Hannibal's beloved city-state, Carthage.

Yet today strategists and military historians continue to study Hannibal's tactics. Guerrilla forces, such as the Vietcong, still use the devices of ambush, terror, and surprise which he demonstrated could be used to demoralize a larger, better-equipped opponent. And America's black militants like to point out that Hannibal, although white, led an invasion army of thousands of dark-skinned warriors into Italy —a land of whites.

For fifteen years Hannibal marched his army across the length and breadth of the Italian peninsula without suffering a major defeat in open combat. He baffled Rome's finest generals, outmaneuvered them, surprised them. Despite the wealth and manpower of Rome, the Carthaginian hero came tantalizingly close to winning his gamble and changing the course of history.

This then is the story of a great leader and of vast world forces in collision. And over all, dominating the scene, broods the solitary, elusive personality of Hannibal.

# CHAPTER 1

# CARTHAGE AND ROME

Hannibal lived one of history's most remarkable lives. Yet it is impossible to understand his career without knowing something about the momentous conflict between Carthage and Rome in which he played such an important role. Therefore before beginning the story of Hannibal, we should pause briefly to describe those two warring city-states.

Carthage was a city in North Africa, near the present site of Tunis. About 750 years before the birth of Jesus the city was founded by the Phoenicians—a Semitic people, like the Biblical Jews.

Ancient legend credits the founding of Carthage to Dido, daughter of the King of Tyre, a kingdom on the narrow strip of eastern Mediterranean coastline which today is the nation of Lebanon. The earliest settlers of Carthage were traders from the Phoenician cities of Tyre and Sidon. They were seeking good farm land and a trading post. Later, Carthage became a way station for voyagers along the route westward to the Pillars of Hercules and beyond.

The seafaring ways of the Phoenician people are described in the Old Testament. Indeed our word "Bible" is derived from the Phoenician port of Biblos. So much paper was shipped from Biblos that the Greeks took their word for "book" from the name of the city. We, in turn, speak of the Bible, or "*the* book."

Because of its location Phoenicia was open to frequent attacks. Its armies never were very strong. But as the fortunes of the Phoenician cities of Tyre and Sidon waned, their Carthaginian colony prospered. Practical and ambitious, the Carthaginians irrigated their soil for planting. They domesticated animals.

However, they were first of all traders. Their caravans knifed south of the Sahara into the African interior, returning with slaves and gold, ivory and elephants. Their galleys journeyed to Britain, to western Europe. They pressed tightly along Africa's Atlantic coast. Fully 2,000 years before the adventurous Portuguese in the school of Prince Henry the Navigator, they were explorers of the Atlantic.

Sometimes the Carthaginians established new trading colonies of their own. But often they simply took over the old Phoenician trading posts along the shores of the Mediterranean—in North Africa and Spain, as well as on Sicily, Sardinia, Malta, and Cyprus.

In time, the Carthaginians came into conflict with another trading people, the Greeks. The Greeks were also looking for ports and farm land. They wanted especially to hold the coasts of southern Italy and western Sicily. In Sicily their expansion met that of the Carthaginians head on. A long and bitter naval war followed. Bloody battles were fought in the waters around Sicily, directly across the Mediterranean from Carthage's splendid home harbor.

Gradually Carthage grew more powerful, its battle fleet more daring. The war continued, but Carthage had the upper hand.

Yet the Carthaginians remained primarily merchants, not fighters. They left most of their fighting to mercenaries —soldiers fighting for pay—drawn from their colonies and from neighboring African states. The armies were led, however, by a few Carthaginian families, such as the Barcids, who took pride in a tradition of military leadership.

Of the mercenary fighters none were more feared than the Numidians—tough desert warriors from what today are the lands of Algeria, Tunisia, and Libya. Numidian horsemen became the high-spirited shock troops of Carthage's army. Their blood-curdling war cry and their ferociousness in hand-to-hand combat were known throughout the ancient Mediterranean world. Today's fierce Berber tribesmen of northern Africa are their descendants.

The Carthaginians turned to war and conquest not as ends in themselves, but to preserve and expand their trade advantages. True, when warships were needed, they were built; when soldiers were needed, they were hired. But Carthage used armed force—along with bribery, diplomacy, and an occasional judicious marriage—mainly to win the trade concessions and peace essential to the conduct of business. In the daily life of Carthage success in business, not war, was the major consideration.

The combination of shrewd commercial dealing and victory on the battlefield was profitable. Carthage's merchants, especially such powerful families as the Hanno clan, became immensely rich. Their homes were like palaces. They adorned themselves in expensive robes edged in the famous Tyrian purple, a dye obtained from murex—a shellfish. They dined exquisitely on delicacies imported from the distant corners of the empire.

The Carthaginians improved their magnificent harbor, encircling it with 440 majestic marble columns. Since Carthage was built on a peninsula, jutting out into the Mediterranean, the leaders of the city had a wall erected on the only approach not surrounded by water. It was of colossal thickness and forty-five feet high. Eventually, two other walls were built behind the first for even greater protection. In the city itself, great stone battlements appeared, alongside grim forbidding towers. Unsmiling and suspicious despite all its luxury, Carthage grew and prospered.

Conquest produced more conquest. As gold and silver flowed into Carthage, especially from the mines of Spain, the Carthaginians organized still more powerful armies. Soon the mercenary camps swarmed with warriors of many tongues, many costumes. Everywhere one could see the audacious Numidian cavalrymen, who rode without saddles and could shoot an arrow at full gallop. The Numidians mingled easily with fighting men from all around the rim of the Mediterranean—men whose only career was war and the taking of loot. There were red-haired Gauls from what are today southern France and northern Italy; fierce, dark Libyans; dashing, romantic slingers from the Balearic Islands —soldiers even more deadly in casting their lead missiles than the ancient Hebrews; stealthy Iberians, the native inhabitants of Spain, who always fought naked from the waist up; and in increasing numbers, the stoically sullen Greeks and Italians who came as Roman deserters.

These were the men who made up the Carthaginian army—a striking force which under Hannibal's leadership would leave an indelible mark on history.

In appearance the Carthaginians as a people resembled the ancient Jews, neighbors of Phoenicia on the eastern shore of the Mediterranean. Their language, too, was something like classical Hebrew. But their religion was strikingly different. They were worshippers of Baal. This is reflected, historian Will Durant points out, in such names as Hasdrubal, "He whose help is Baal," and Hannibal, the very "Grace of Baal." Infant sacrifice was a regular part of the religion. Live infants, usually the children of the poor, but sometimes of the rich, were rolled from the extended arms of an idol into a fire below. It is said that as many as 300 infants might be cast into the fire in a single day. For their sacrifice to be acceptable, the mothers were required to look on calmly, betraying not the slightest trace of emotion. Compassion never was a quality highly prized by the demanding nature deities of Hannibal's city.

Little is known about Carthaginian government. A popularly elected assembly chose two Shofets or magistrates. Most probably the real power of the state rested with a Council, or Senate, of 300 elders. It was they who determined how long a military commander would remain in the field. It was also the Council which decided how much money would be sent to a field commander, how well he would be supplied, whether he would be reinforced.

Almost always the Council's decisions were based on what would be most beneficial to the business and commercial interests of the home city. Generals were the servants of the merchants, not their masters. This great concern with the getting and keeping of money profited Carthage in the short run. In the long run it would prove fatal.

Just as Carthage was beginning to feel safe from the danger of Greek sea power in the western Mediterranean a new threat arose—Rome. Roman merchants often landed in Sicily, which the Carthaginians considered their special trading area. Sometimes the cities of Sicily asked help from Rome against Carthage. For a time, the Carthaginians tried to make treaties of agreement with Rome. But tension grew. Finally there was war.

Three wars were fought between Carthage and Rome. They are known as the Punic Wars, since *Poeni* was the Latin word for Phoenicians.

The Roman people had begun as farmers, living in an obscure community beside the lower Tiber River. But they were also fine soldiers, superbly organized for combat. By swallowing up their weaker neighbors and then repelling foreign invasions they gradually absorbed most of the Italian peninsula.

In 264 B.C., when the first of its three wars with Carthage began, Rome was the underdog; it appeared to have little chance of winning. The city on the Tiber was still rude in its manners and had had no experience in warfare outside Italy. The Romans, unlike their Carthaginian rivals, began with no fleet of swift quinqueremes—great warships with five banks of oars; they could not depend on a massive flow of precious metals from provincial mines to pay their armies; they could not, like their African opponents, collect some 12,000 talents—more than $43,000,000—in annual tribute from subject states.

At the beginning of the First Punic War, however, Rome had certain important advantages. It had solid control of all Italy south of the Po River valley. Its resources were not extended as thinly as those of Carthage. Its army was composed of free men, mostly landowners; so too, in most cases, were the armies of its allies. The term during which men might be called for service was long, from ages seventeen to forty-five. Training was rigorous, duty a serious matter. The penalty for insubordination, cowardice, or desertion almost always was death. But the rewards were also great—honors and booty, perhaps a political career.

Weighing heavily with the Roman citizen, too, was the privilege of serving one's own homeland; for this intangible value the free Roman showed himself far more willing to risk his life in distant battles than the wealthy Carthaginian. Roman Senators, when faced with seemingly certain defeat, contributed their own money and property to help save the state. The Carthaginian elders, selfish and shortsighted, never equalled that kind of defiance and self-sacrifice.

During the Punic Wars Rome was a rising power. Its people were not brilliant and keen-witted like the Greeks. Rather they were practical, conservative, stolid—not very receptive to new ideas. They were also completely devoted to their city. Like the dogged, tenacious British in later centuries, the Romans were at their best when things looked darkest.

By the year 264 B.C. the Romans had decided that it was in their interest to extend their control to northern Sicily, just across the narrows from Italy. They also felt obliged to live up to their agreements—pledges to provide aid and protection for their allies in time of trouble. Carthage was in the way of Roman expansion and was a source of fear on the part of Rome's southern Italian allies.

Meanwhile, Carthage believed that it must defend at all costs its supply routes and its markets for trade. If it did not stop Rome's expansion, it would eventually find its trade choked off by Roman military might—and perhaps later by Roman commercial growth.

So the interests and ambitions of the two great Mediterranean powers came into direct conflict. With neither side willing to compromise, a clash was almost inevitable. The struggle which followed was to be a turning point in the history of Western man.

# CHAPTER 2

# HAMILCAR AND SON

Hannibal was born in 247 B.C. In that year his father, Hamilcar Barca, was made supreme commander of all Carthaginian forces, both on land and sea. Barca meant "Thunderbolt," and the vigorous, exciting Hamilcar fit the name well.

The Barcid clan was unusual in Carthage. Although the family had become wealthy through commerce, they retained their aristocratic position by serving as military leaders. They were exceptional in another way, too. Consistently the Barcids lined up as defenders of the masses of the Carthaginian people against the rich commercial classes —against conservative families, including the powerful Hanno clan. This rivalry made many leaders of the Carthaginian Council suspicious of every request for funds that Hamilcar, and later Hannibal, made from the battlefield. The Council, dominated by conservatives, never quite trusted the Barcids.

By the time Hamilcar became commander of the army, Carthage and Rome had been engaged in the first of the Punic Wars for seventeen years. Battles had been fought at sea throughout the Mediterranean, and on land in Sicily and in Africa. Exhausted, neither side had been able to deliver a knockout blow. The war dragged on indecisively.

All of this changed when Hamilcar took command. He assembled a small fleet of warships and proceeded to swoop down on the Italian coast. Repeatedly he struck in lightning-like raids against Roman outposts, seized booty, and vanished. The Romans could not stop him; he was hurting them gravely.

Hamilcar pleaded for money and supplies from the Carthaginian Council so that he could smash Rome into submission and end the war. The Senators refused, arguing that if his success was so great, he could surely manage to live off the Roman countryside. Besides, why should they spend more money than necessary to help Hamilcar Barca, a man who held merchants in such contempt?

Meanwhile, the Romans girded for a final desperate effort. They stripped themselves bare of funds to build a great fleet of 200 ships. Then they launched a surprise naval attack at the Aegadian Islands, off Sicily. The Carthaginian navy was destroyed. Without a fleet to protect its trade, Carthage was soon helpless. It could not afford to pay its mercenary soldiers nor rebuild its fleet. In 241 B.C. Carthage sued for peace.

The peace treaty called for an indemnity to Rome of 440 talents a year for ten years. In addition, Carthage had to surrender Sicily and promise not to interfere with Roman trade in the Mediterranean.

After making peace, Hamilcar returned to Carthage. There he found some of the city's hired soldiers in open revolt. When the treasury was full, the greedy Senators had tried to save money by not paying the soldiers; many were not paid for months. Then, drained of resources by defeat at the hands of Rome, the elders were unable to pay at all.

Carthage's rich merchants begged Hamilcar to save the city. The mercenary troops had placed it under siege, intent on overthrowing the Punic government. Hamilcar hesitated. Among the rebels were many who had served him faithfully.

Finally he decided that, despite the stupidity of the Council, his loyalty to Carthage came first. When the Council reluctantly offered him command of an army, he raised the siege and pursued the mercenaries into the mountains.

The infuriated soldiers retreated before Hamilcar. But seeing their capture and death as certain, they paused long enough to take revenge on Carthage. Herding some 700 Carthaginian prisoners together, the rebels cut off their captives' hands and feet, broke their legs, and cast them, still alive, into a common grave.

When at last the mercenaries surrendered, Hamilcar had the leader of the revolt crucified and several hundred of the soldiers crushed to death under the feet of elephants.

In the interval, the Romans took advantage of Carthage's agony to seize the islands of Corsica and Sardinia and to demand an additional cash indemnity from the defenseless African state. Although the war was over and the peace treaty signed, the Carthaginians had no choice but to agree. Carthage raised the extra money and recognized Rome's control over the two strategic islands. But the land-hungry, ambitious Italians had not dealt honorably with their opponents. And now Carthage thirsted for revenge.

During the revolt and siege of Carthage by the mercenaries, Hannibal, then only five years old, had spent many days at his father's side in the encampment of loyal troops inside the besieged city. It had been an important time in Hannibal's life. Every day in camp was an education for him. He lived among colorful warriors from many countries. Some were scarcely removed from savagery; others the products of advanced civilizations.

Eagerly Hannibal absorbed their languages, customs, superstitions. He noticed the way his father roared commands and curses at the men, yet how he won their loyalty with fairness and rewards. Once the reward might be a few tinkling pieces of silver, another time permission to keep a sprightly wench plucked from a burning enemy stronghold. Always Hamilcar gave the men something to bind them to him.

Hannibal, bright and impressionable, watched and learned. He took in the life of the camp and came to understand the lusty, robust ways of soldiers. Then, when the mercenaries' revolt was suppressed and Carthage once again safe, young Hannibal was sent back to live in his father's luxurious palace.

It was another world. Hannibal was surrounded by fawning servants and tutors. Purple-robed courtiers moved silently through the corridors. Everywhere the boy saw sophisticated men and women bedecked with jewelry and smelling of musky perfume.

He could look out over orchards and gardens, a colonnaded square lined with Greek sculpture, a teeming city bustling with the sights and sounds of the bazaar. Still, with all of this, Hannibal never forgot his early experiences in the military encampment.

Hamilcar's personal hatred of the Romans knew no bounds. Eager for revenge, he proposed a major attack on Rome. It was to be launched from Carthage's old trading settlements in Spain, especially the ancient city of Gades (the modern Cadiz). Hamilcar would rely for money on the iron and silver mines of the region. Then, aided by the native Spanish allies he planned to attract, he would begin a devastating attack on the Roman heartland itself.

To please the Carthaginian Council, Hamilcar presented the first stage of his plan as one for expansion of their territories in Spain. Even so, the Council gave him far less money than he said he needed and only a small army.

Nevertheless, Hamilcar set out at once for Spain. With him was Hannibal. This was just four years after the revolt of the mercenaries and Hannibal was only nine years old. Legend has it that before accompanying his father to Spain,

Hannibal swore a sacred oath in the Temple of Dido. With his hand on a sacrificial lamb killed by Hamilcar himself, young Hannibal pledged undying enmity for Rome. Never, he declared, would he submit to Roman rule. Never would he cease his efforts to crush the Roman state.

From his youth Hannibal was groomed for a single task: to destroy Rome. Only by stopping Rome's expansion, he was taught, could Carthage's people and its commercial empire survive. The first stories Hannibal heard were about his father's brave defiance of Roman power. He was schooled like a gentleman to love Greek philosophy and poetry and to know Homer. He spoke many languages. Yet his tutors missed no opportunity to remind him of the cruelty and treachery of the Italian foe. Hatred of Rome was his most important lesson.

Hamilcar's Spanish campaign moved swiftly. In a stunning series of victories he recaptured many of the Spanish towns which had deserted Carthage during the First Punic War. He mined the wealth of the Sierra Morena—also known as the Silver Mountains. And he formed alliances with the native Iberian tribesmen, with the Celts, and with the Celtiberians—a rugged people created by intermarriage among the Celts and Iberians. At the time the Celts roamed the coasts of Spain, as well as territories both north and south of the Alps; some had already begun what was to be an historically important migration toward northern Europe.

For nine years Hamilcar Barca patiently organized the peoples of the Iberian peninsula—modern Spain and Portugal—preparing for the day when he would again lead his forces against the Roman legions. Once, Roman envoys visited him. They asked about the increased Carthaginian activity in Spain.

Hamilcar answered evasively. Was it not necessary, he suggested, to have some source of revenue to pay the indemnity demanded by Rome? Busy with wars against the

Gauls on both sides of the Alps, the Romans had little time to fret about once-defeated Carthage. Eventually, however, Rome won a promise from the Carthaginians that Punic armies would not extend their actions north of the Ebro River.

The promise did not keep Hamilcar from his vital task of gathering recruits among the hardy Spanish tribesmen. Sometimes he persuaded, sometimes he used force, but his army steadily grew. Helping him in the delicate work of recruiting were his "lion's brood," as he called them—his three sons, Hannibal, Hasdrubal, and Mago, and his son-in-law, another Hasdrubal. Gradually the free-roving and undisciplined Spanish warriors were sharpened by the Barcid family into a seasoned fighting force capable of great endurance and daring offensive strikes.

Many tribesmen were won over by Hannibal and were bound to him by a personal oath of loyalty. Especially among the Celtiberians such an oath was considered unbreakable for life.

In these years Hannibal's character was formed. Childhood turned to adolescence and manhood as the Carthaginian warrior roamed the hills and valleys of Andalusia. Later, in Hannibal's casual dress and his admiration for the unorthodox daring of Spanish cavalry, there were hints of just how important those years in Spain had been to him.

Perhaps the bold young African began to see Iberia as a personal possession over which he might one day rule. Perhaps he saw mirrored in the vigorous Spanish people the independence, resourcefulness and command of every faculty that he worked so hard to develop in himself.

For his wife, Hannibal chose Imilce, a Spanish princess said to have been of Greek descent. Her ancestors had been among the many Greeks who established trading colonies along the southern coast of Spain.

Legend has it that through all the years of their separation, almost from the honeymoon, Hannibal was faithful to her. Yet any authentic knowledge of Imilce remains forever lost in the shadows of history. We are certain that she and Hannibal had a son. But it is not known whether she or the boy survived to greet the great warrior when he returned at last to Carthage from the campaigns which won him lasting fame. No letters which the two may have exchanged are mentioned by the Roman historians to whom we owe what little information remains of the elusive Imilce. Imilce's personality, even more than Hannibal's, is a mystery.

Hamilcar Barca did not live to see Hannibal's marriage. One day, with Hannibal riding at his side, Hamilcar was ambushed and slain by Spanish tribesmen.

Hannibal escaped. With the rest of the "lion's brood" he pledged to carry on his father's vendetta against Rome. The Carthaginian army officers elected "Hasdrubal the Splendid," Hamilcar's son-in-law, as their commander, and for eight more years Carthage labored to complete its conquest of Spain.

Hasdrubal the Splendid built a magnificent city, Carthago Nova—the modern Cartagena; he formed more tribal alliances; he extracted more wealth from the mines.

In 221 B.C. Hasdrubal met the fate of his father-in-law; he was assassinated. This time the army elected as its chief the eldest son of Hamilcar—Hannibal. He was then twenty-six years old, almost all of those years spent in camp.

The Carthaginian Senate accepted the army's choice of Hannibal as commander. And why not? All was going well in New Carthage. Besides, word of Hannibal's election was transmitted to Africa along with welcome gifts of gold and silver and hides. Still, the Senators knew surprisingly little about the enigmatic soldier who, at the age of nine, had first sailed with his father from Carthage for the Spanish provinces.

According to the Roman historian, Livy, when Hannibal took command in Spain the soldiers eagerly flocked to him:

> . . . for they imagined Hamilcar in his
> youth was restored to them; they
> noticed the same vigor in his frame,
> the same fire in his eyes, the same
> features and expression in his face.

But Hannibal was no mere tintype of his father; he was a leader in his own right. Livy—no friend of Carthage—relates that Hannibal had steeled his body to hardship. He could endure heat and cold alike, rarely showing fatigue; he ate only what he needed and drank wine sparingly. Working day and night, sleeping only for brief intervals, he was capable of prodigious feats. It is said that he did not rest until the needs of his men were met, and then not in the softness of a tent but on the ground, close to the sentries, draped only in a lion-skin cape.

His clothing, like his men's, was of coarse cloth, unadorned by any insignia of rank, although he loved fine horses and splendidly jeweled weapons. Strong, tall for a Carthaginian, Hannibal was known as a remarkable athlete. He was a fine horseman, a swift runner, a skillful huntsman.

Once Hannibal's army was stopped by a flooded river. Throwing himself into the roaring torrent, he swam to the other side and then helped the others across. In combat, says Livy, he was "the first to enter the battle, the last to abandon the field." For sheer physical courage and stamina few commanders in history compare with Hannibal.

Yet he was essentially a man of thought. He enjoyed the reading and writing of history. He saw war as a supreme exercise of the intellect, calling upon the general's imagination and diplomatic skill, his capacity to fit local events into a world picture. Hannibal trusted few men with his thoughts, preferring to listen and learn. Often he would sit by the campfire through the night, hearing tales spun by passing travelers, curious always about other people—their customs, modes of warfare, ideas. Hannibal pondered all that he heard, turned it over in the privacy of his mind, speculated.

His conclusions he revealed to no one, not even his beloved brothers, Hasdrubal and Mago.

Long before the study of psychology was formalized, Hannibal was a practitioner of the art. He applied his father's lessons in the use of reward and punishment as tools in the handling of men. In the field he gauged the mind and emotional habits of opposing commanders as closely as the terrain of a battlefield. Thus his great victories were won more by brainpower than manpower, more by stealth than strength. Badly outnumbered by the Romans, he usually had little choice but to try to out-think them and throw them off balance psychologically.

Because of the odds against him, Hannibal needed to draw upon all of the wit, the guile, and the tremendous willpower which were his heritage.

# CHAPTER 3

# ACROSS
# THE ALPS

Almost as soon as Hannibal took command of the Carthaginian army he was faced with a crisis. He learned from his spies that Roman armies on both sides of the Alps were finally succeeding in their campaigns against the Gauls. Hannibal also learned that Italian ships were being fitted for new action. He suspected they would try to help Saguntum, a Roman client city—a city under Rome's protection—on the Spanish coast. If he did not move quickly, Rome might dominate the western Mediterranean as it already did the Adriatic and Tyrrhenian seas. (*See* map, p. 26.)

When the Saguntians attacked tribes friendly to Carthage, Hannibal had the excuse he needed. He placed Saguntum under siege. Roman agents protested, first to Hannibal then to the Carthaginian Council, but to no avail. While negotiations continued, Hannibal captured the town and sold its defenders into slavery.

Just what happened after this is obscure, but sooner or later Rome sent a delegation of five high-ranking ministers to Carthage, demanding that Hannibal be surrendered to them. It was an ultimatum. Either Hannibal would be surrendered or there would be war.

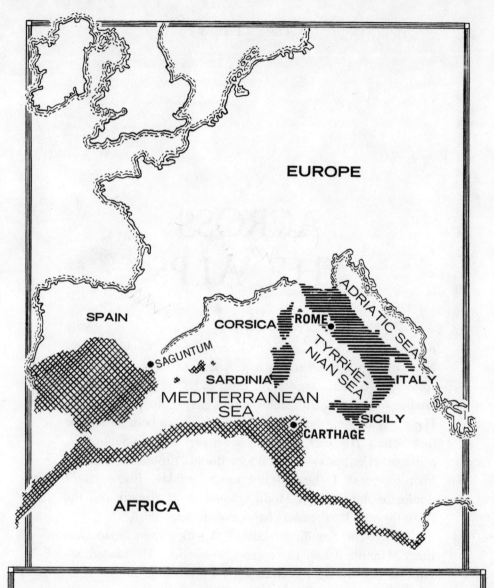

EUROPE

SPAIN

CORSICA

ROME

ADRIATIC SEA

SAGUNTUM

TYRRHĒ-
NIAN SEA

ITALY

SARDINIA

MEDITERRANEAN
SEA

SICILY

CARTHAGE

AFRICA

# Roman and Carthaginian Dominions when Hannibal Took Command

 CARTHAGINIAN
DOMINIONS

ROMAN
DOMINIONS

Would Carthage give in? The city elders had yielded to Roman pressure before. The First Punic War had shown them less than resolute when faced with superior force; they had surrendered Corsica and Sardinia without a fight; they had promised Rome to remain south of the Ebro. Further, a strong Carthaginian peace party, headed by the statesman Hanno, looked to long-term friendship with Rome. Hanno saw the African interior as a more fruitful field for expansion —one much easier to exploit.

But Hannibal's successes had undermined the position of the peace party and made the Senators, for once, more reckless. "Was not Rome in violation of its treaty?" asked the Carthaginian elders. After all, they pointed out, Saguntum lay 100 miles *south* of the Ebro, not north of it. Was it proper for the Romans to conclude an alliance inside the Punic sphere? From a strictly legal standpoint the Carthaginians were correct.

It is said that at this point Fabius,* the stately, dignified leader of the Roman delegation, slowly rose to his feet, tightly clasping about him the traditional white Roman robe.

"Enough of this wearisome talk," said Fabius. "I hold within this fold of my toga war or peace. Which do you choose?"

The Punic ministers withdrew to consider the ultimatum. Returning to the chamber, they cannily announced that the choice (and the responsibility for war) was not theirs but the Romans.

"Then," answered Fabius, "it shall be war!"

"Yes, war!" shouted the Carthaginian elders in reply. "War! We accept it!"

Without further discussion the diplomats filed from the room.

Swiftly the news of renewed war between the two

---

* This was not the same Fabius who later gained fame as Hannibal's opponent on the battlefield, although both were members of the Fabian clan.

superstates, Carthage and Rome, spread through the Mediterranean world. Clearly, this would not be another struggle for commercial advantage, but a conflict for survival.

Rome expected to defeat Carthage quickly. One expeditionary force would pin down Hannibal's army in Spain while another struck at the African homeland. Commanders were dispatched to these fronts at a leisurely pace, their victory considered only a matter of time.

But while the Romans slowly collected their forces, Hannibal seized the initiative. The Punic commander grasped the totality of the situation: Rome had naval superiority; Rome had an inexhaustible supply of manpower. His only hope was to strike at the heart of his enemy before the overwhelming Italian advantages could be brought to bear on him. In Italy, thought Hannibal, some of Rome's shaky allies could be counted on to join him; the Gauls, thirsting for revenge, would welcome the opportunity. Anticipating the declaration of war, Hannibal prepared his armies. The moment he learned that it was official, he was ready to march.

Before setting out, he bundled Imilce, his wife, and his young son onto a ship bound for Carthage. Then he embarked immediately on his historic campaign.

In May, 218 B.C., with an army of perhaps 50,000 men— a column which would have been six miles long—Hannibal crossed the Ebro. He was now in Roman territory. In the ranks were men he had trained: tough, courageous, experienced fighters with supreme confidence in their leader. He could demand of them unlimited effort, tremendous endurance in the face of hardship.

From the beginning he had to make just such demands. Forcing his way through the Pyrenees, he was harassed all the way by Gallic allies of the Roman client city, Marseilles. Finally he reached the Rhone, where he was seen by advance patrols of the Roman force sent to hold him at bay. To delay was unthinkable since it was now late summer and the autumn snows would clog the Alpine passes. A costly and time-consuming battle could doom his plans.

Without warning, a hostile Gallic war party appeared, barring the way.

Hannibal improvised brilliantly. While holding the native tribesmen at arm's length, he sent part of his army northward to cross the Rhone farther upstream. After fording it easily, they came upon the Gauls from behind, putting them to flight. With hastily constructed boats and rafts Hannibal ferried his men and a herd of forty prize war elephants across the fast-moving river. When Publius Cornelius Scipio, the Roman Consul, arrived in Gaul with his army, the elusive Hannibal had vanished.

Scipio, astonished, realized now that Hannibal had something far more audacious in mind than merely conquering the Rhone Valley. Incredible as it seemed, reasoned Scipio, the African leader must be intent on crossing the Alps and invading Italy. Leaving most of his army in Spain, Scipio departed by ship, planning to intercept the survivors of Hannibal's Alpine crossing with a small force and exterminate them—if, indeed, there were to be any survivors. Meanwhile, the Roman army already embarked for Africa was recalled to Italy, just in case Hannibal did the impossible and conquered Rome's "outer walls."

In October, 218 B.C., the only people who knew the Alps were the Gauls. Desperately needing guides, Hannibal turned to two friendly Gallic tribes, the Boii and the Insubres. In exchange for Carthage's help in their local political squabbles, the natives eagerly consented to lead the Punic armies to the summit of the mountains.

Hearing that native tribes had mastered the Alps many times before in the autumn was of some comfort to Hannibal's men. Understandably, a current of uneasiness ran through the line of march as young men, far from their homes, gazed upward at the bleak, awesome peaks, already tipped with snow.

The elderly Boii chieftain spoke to the men of other journeys his people had made over the heights in his own lifetime and in the days of his ancestors. Then, according to Livy, Hannibal faced the officers of all the nations in his army. He reminded them of the great journey they had already made and how close they were to the fertile valleys of Italy. Without making light of the great ordeal looming before them, he diverted their attention away from their fears to the real problems of the passage.

"These are but mountains, not unlike other mountains you have climbed," said the great Carthaginian soothingly. "Would you rather return to your homes and families never having beheld the enemy? Ahead lies the wealth and booty of Rome; behind, only our pursuers."

With words of confidence Hannibal dismissed the men, ordering them to make ready for the ominous ascent.

The fearful climb to the summit began. For much of the way Hannibal's army, numbed by cold, was harassed by hardy Allobroges warriors. Skilled mountain fighters, the Allobroges scented loot. Time and again Hannibal was forced to pause and send patrols after the marauders, who were drawn like jackals by his inviting train of supply carts and handsome animals. Finally discouraged, they were left behind as Hannibal led his band still higher along the winding mountain trails.

On the fourth day a delegation of smiling natives, dressed in ragged animal pelts, greeted Hannibal, proclaiming friendship and offering to lead the Carthaginians to the pass they sought. Instead, the tribesmen led them into a blind ravine. From nowhere, hidden warriors rose up, and with blood-curdling yells, let loose a crushing avalanche of rocks and boulders onto the heads of the African force. Scores of pack animals and hundreds of men were killed. For a time the army was split in two by the cascading stones. Only Hannibal's coolness and presence of mind prevented panic. With the troops of his rear guard he warded off the surprise assault. Thwarted in their hopes of an easy victory, the treacherous mountain men reluctantly fled. But they had done serious damage to the army. Many soldiers in the line of march were seriously wounded and had to be carried.

Late in October, after a nine-day ascent, Hannibal reached the summit of the pass. He had no choice but to rest his exhausted army. In drifting snow and howling winds, Hannibal and his men bivouacked in the open for two days and two nights. No longer was there wood for the fires or food for the animals. Sick men collapsed and died. The elephants, unaccustomed to the cold, were covered with tent canvas, but they suffered greatly. Stray men and animals, sometimes whole units which had been cut off from the main line of march, straggled fitfully into the camp.

On the morning of the third day, Hannibal gathered his officers around him at the rim of the summit. Raising his arm, he pointed to the south, toward Italy. There, he said, would be green fields and bubbling streams, the marble cities of Italy, warm nights, women. Wine and gold awaited them below at the end of their descent to the Po Valley.

The descent was steep, the trail narrow and icy. Along the route hundreds of men slipped over the precipice to their deaths in the gorges an eternity below. Animals became mired in the thick snow or, weakened by lack of grazing, simply died by the side of the trail. Heads bowed against the chilling winds, the long line of marchers slowly curled its way downward toward the valley.

Once, a landslide of snow covered the path, making it impossible to move the supply carts through. Hannibal had his engineers cut a new road and line it with timber. Approaching the foot of the trail, a rockslide proved even more troublesome. According to Livy's account, the ingenious Carthaginian leader treated the rocks with vinegar—probably old wine—and then applied fire to them. Weakened by the acid content of the vinegar, the rocks were far easier for the soldiers to crumble with their picks. Hannibal had learned of this trick in his studies of Greek science, but to his men it seemed nothing less than magical. It made him appear even more godlike to them.

Finally, in early November, Hannibal's army burst forth onto the plains of northern Italy. Exhausted, dirty, their clothing in shreds, the soldiers rested in the villages of the Boii, who had befriended them on the other side of the mountains.

Hannibal had crossed the mountains in seventeen days. His casualties were enormous, perhaps higher than 20,000 since his departure from the Rhone. Still, his army, now reduced to only 26,000 men, was intact. The morale of the survivors was high as they gathered around warm campfires and drank from the clear waters of streams rushing to join the Po River.

The accomplishment of the ever-confident Carthaginian general was formidable. He had led a civilized army with all of its supplies and war animals through the Pyrenees, across the Rhone, and over the Alps—all in less than five months! He had eluded the Roman army and brushed aside the fierce resistance of barbarian tribesmen. By the sheer strength of his will he had deposited a compact, superbly disciplined force of killers at the very doorstep of Rome.

In the annals of military history the lightning march of Hannibal across the Alps is considered one of the great strokes of strategy. It placed the enormously more powerful Romans on the defensive. It forced them to defend their own home territory. It upset completely their plans for a leisurely invasion of Africa and an easy victory there. Instead of victory, the Romans were face to face with the uncertain prospect of conflict and possible defeat.

Soldiers of many nations—all enemies of Rome united under Hannibal—lay encamped on the plains of northern

Italy. Slowly they recovered their strength, honed their weapons. The winter snows and the Roman legions posted on the other side of the Alps made retreat impossible for Hannibal. He summoned his men together and spoke to them, telling them what most already suspected. Only one route really remained open, the one they had come to follow —the road to Rome.

CHAPTER 4

# THE ROAD
# TO ROME

Hannibal had successfully crossed the Alps. Still, the Roman
Senate was not unduly alarmed. Its spies told gruesome tales
of the heavy Punic casualties. The Romans knew that Hannibal's retreat was cut off. And they were aware that he had
only limited siege machinery. He would either have to
persuade some Italian city to open its gates to him or,
without a base of operations, be forced to live off the land
from day to day in order to feed his men. Moreover, since
Rome controlled the sea, Hannibal could depend on only a
trickle of reinforcements from Carthage. He would have to
augment his ranks by enlisting Italian defectors or see his
force gradually melt away in the normal course of operations. Rome, on the other hand, could call on the manpower
reserves of its own population and its Italian allies for a
total force of some 770,000 men.

Finally, the Romans also felt confident because of the
well-earned reputation of their legions. The Roman army
was a superb fighting machine, its men known for their iron
discipline and unflinching obedience to orders. Legionaries
did not panic in combat. The city on the Tiber had good
reason to feel secure.

Two months later the situation was spectacularly different. In that brief time the tiny Carthaginian force conquered all of northern Italy and was streaking south, the road to Rome completely open before it.

In their otherwise reasonable calculations, the Roman military had failed to take into account the tactical genius of Hannibal.

When the Roman army, led by Publius Cornelius Scipio the Elder, first met the Carthaginians in November, 218 B.C., little more than a cavalry duel resulted. The skirmish served, however, to shake the confidence of the Romans in their invincibility. Scipio had raced from Gaul to greet Hannibal in the Alpine foothills. When the Roman legions caught sight of Carthaginian advance units near the Ticinus River, they immediately moved forward to do battle.

Instead of responding with his infantry in the accepted manner of the time, Hannibal sent his Numidian cavalry darting to the flanks of the Roman legions. Charging at full speed, the Africans quickly emerged at the Romans' rear, hurling their javelins into the astonished third rank of legionaries who turned in confusion to meet them.

In the heat of the battle, Scipio fell to the ground wounded. He was rescued by his own son, Publius Cornelius Scipio the Younger, later to become known as Scipio Africanus.

Surrounded, the Romans tightened their formation and managed to retreat in good order to their fortified camp, carrying their wounded with them. Hannibal made no attempt to follow.

Scipio the Elder withdrew to a line of well-entrenched positions between the two strong points of Placentia and Cremona. These were two recently founded Roman colonies near the Po River, set up for protection against the Gauls. Still weak from his wounds and cautious after the lesson of the Ticinus, Scipio proposed to go into winter quarters. Just then, however, he was jointed by the Consul, T. Sempronius Longus, who led the army originally dispatched to conquer Africa. Sempronius lacked both patience and combat experience. He was, moreover, highly ambitious. A victory over the dreaded Carthaginians would win him the popularity in Rome for which he hungered.

It did not take Hannibal long to learn that there was disagreement between the two Roman leaders. Information gathered by his intelligence chief, a mysterious African officer named Carthalo, proved amazingly accurate. Weighing the Latin mentality, Hannibal gambled that Sempronius Longus would have his way; the Romans would fight.

Hannibal envisioned the outcome of the battle before a single sword was drawn. First he rode out to inspect the land on his side of the Trebia River, which separated the two hostile armies. A sunken stream-bed, heavily matted with tangled underbrush, caught his glance. That night he carefully concealed in the thick foliage 2,000 of his bravest soldiers—men he trusted completely. They were under command of his own brother, Mago.

Before dawn, Hannibal fed his men a generous meal and distributed to each a full ration of oil to protect their limbs against the bitter cold December morning. Then, while his infantry waited, Hannibal sent his Numidian cavalry to entice the Romans into combat.

Sempronius Longus leaped at the bait. Hastily awakening his men, and not troubling to feed them, he began to chase the Numidian horsemen. He plunged after them into the chest-high waters of the frigid Trebia.

As the major force of the Roman legions emerged from the stream—hungry, soaked to the skin, fatigued by their difficult march—they were set upon by Hannibal's troops. Infantry and slingers hit them in the center of their line, and heavy cavalry struck at their flanks. The horses of the Romans bolted in fear before the charging African elephants —the heavy tanks of their day. Both ends of the Italian line bowed in toward the center.

By noon the Romans had struggled from the mud of the Trebia only to be surprised from the rear. The troops

Hannibal had concealed in the sunken stream-bed now emerged from hiding and struck the decisive blow of the battle.

Chaos reigned. Hundreds of Romans were cut down trying to escape across the river; others died on the field, not knowing what had happened; whole units surrendered, giving up their standards bearing the famed Roman eagle and Senate emblem. Still, the hard-core Roman center, some 10,000 strong, rallied to fight its way out of the trap. With stragglers trailing after them, they retreated successfully to Placentia and then retired to Cremona.

On the bloody field of the Trebia they left behind more than 20,000 of their comrades, either killed or captured.

Hannibal chose not to pursue the enemy, carefully avoiding losses to his small army. Instead he cultivated the friendship of the Gallic chieftains who ceremoniously visited his tent, eager now to pay him court after his two victories. Hannibal feasted them and patiently explained how great would be their gains if the Romans were defeated and the Gauls again became masters of northern Italy as once they had been. The barbarian leaders drank deeply of fine Punic wines and with great emotion and ferocity pledged support to their African host. Eventually, despite the extravagant words, fewer than 10,000 undisciplined Gauls joined Hannibal's ranks.

Two months passed. The Carthaginians began to grow restless in winter quarters on the Po. With the supply of food dwindling, their village hosts grew uneasy. Would it not be wise, the village elders asked tactfully, for the brave Punic warriors to move south to Etruria and Campania where the nights were warm and the harvests rich?

Hannibal was concerned, too, but for a different reason. Carthalo warned him that the Romans were feverishly raising new levies of troops, mobilizing an army which, by spring, might be too strong for him.

His first move was to free all of his prisoners from

the cities allied to Rome. He asked them to return to their homes and spread the word that Hannibal had come to Italy not to enslave them but to free them from the yoke of Rome.

Next the Carthaginian army moved southward in what was to have been a short cut. But the route was difficult. Squeezing through a little-used Apennine pass, Hannibal's troops soon found themselves slogging across flooded marshland and swamps. For three days and nights they had to march through water. When the pack animals fell in the mud and collapsed, the men tried to stand on top of their bodies to keep out of the water.

Hannibal, swathed in blankets, his head throbbing with pain, rode atop the only surviving elephant. He had some sort of eye disease. The wisest of his Carthaginian physicians could do nothing for him. Eventually he recovered, but he lost the sight of one eye.

Emerging in Etruria, homeland of the Eutruscans—once Rome's great enemy but now a close ally—Hannibal cut a wide swath of destruction. His path was marked by the fires of burning Etrurian villages. This was done for two reasons: first, to destroy the confidence of the native population in Rome's ability to protect them; second, to tempt the legions into a decisive battle.

After the defeat of Sempronius Longus, the Roman people had elected another plebeian Consul* to replace him— Caius Flaminius Nepos. Flaminius was a man of considerable ability. But this Roman commander had one fatal weakness—overconfidence.

Early in the summer of 217 B.C. Flaminius set out in ardent pursuit of the Punic armies. A bevy of slave dealers followed in his wake, equipped with carts and iron manacles to haul away defeated Carthaginians. Many poor Romans

---

* Two consuls were elected annually; one from the patricians (upper-class Romans), the other from the plebeians (lower-class Romans).

viewed the coming battle as an opportunity to acquire slaves and become wealthy.

Meanwhile, Hannibal conjured still another trap for his enemies. This time the tactic was ambush. The scene was a narrow road closely hugging the shores of Lake Trasimene. For a considerable distance the road ran snugly between the lake and low-lying hills, making an extremely narrow passageway.

As usual, on the eve of the battle Hannibal carefully placed his men. In the hills overlooking the roadway he concealed cavalry (horsemen always comprised approximately one-third of his strength) interspersed with spearmen and slingers; archers were strung out at the flanks.

The next morning a heavy mist still hung over the road as Flaminius and a force of 40,000 Romans set out. On higher ground, Hannibal's men were above the mist and could see each other perfectly. The Romans could barely follow the trail.

At Hannibal's signal, the attack began. All of his forces leaped forward simultaneously, falling out of the heights as if from nowhere upon the unsuspecting legions. Many of the Romans were killed at once. The rest found it impossible to take defensive positions in the narrow passageway. Carthaginian horsemen poured into the road at the front and rear of the Roman line of march, sealing off any chance of escape.

Panic broke out in the Roman ranks. Fearful, screaming men clawed and gouged each other in a blind scramble to survive. With no place to flee, relates Livy, thousands waded into the lake until only their heads remained above the water. There they were methodically cut down by pursuing Carthaginians on horseback. The bloody butchery continued for three hours.

By mid-morning when the sun burned off the mist, most of the Roman army had disappeared. Flaminius was dead. An advance unit of 2,000 men, which had marched through before the attack began, was later surrounded and captured. Scarcely 1,000 Romans escaped from the disaster of Lake Trasimene to tell their story in the Forum.

Hannibal had broken the vaunted discipline of the Roman legion. He had totally destroyed an army and taken perhaps as many as 15,000 prisoners.

In Rome, a brief announcement was made by the pro-praetor, M. Pomponius. "We have been defeated," he said, "in a great battle."

The African wizard, Hannibal, could no longer be regarded as little more than a barbarian invader to be dealt with by the customary procedures. Lake Trasimene was less than 100 miles from Rome.

A frightened crowd of citizens, many of them women, gathered expectantly at the northern gates of Rome to learn the fate of loved ones and friends. To them at least it must have seemed that the battle for Italy was over. When would the battle for Rome itself begin?

# CHAPTER 5

# HANNIBAL AT HIS ZENITH

Hannibal did not march on Rome. His army probably numbered no more than 50,000 men; he still lacked a base of supply; and the walled cities of central Italy—even after Trasimene—held out against him. Besides, relief armies from other parts of Italy could be summoned easily to lift a siege of Rome.

Instead of marching directly on Rome, Hannibal contented himself with recrossing the Apennine Mountains, which divide the boot-shaped Italian peninsula like a long spinal cord. He rested his army along the eastern coast of the boot, allowing the men to enjoy the waters of the Adriatic Sea. Then slowly the Carthaginians moved south into the rich farmlands of the Roman province known as Apulia.

Hannibal realized that if ever he were to defeat Rome it would not be with his small army alone. War was only one way to achieve his ends. Diplomacy was another. Just as he had persuaded some of the Gauls to join him, he must persuade Rome's Italian allies. The Roman confederation must be broken and the people of the Italian peninsula turned against their Roman masters.

For this to happen Hannibal had to demonstrate to those people that a Roman defeat was in their interest. This he proposed to do by judicious use of the iron hand in the velvet glove. He continued to release any non-Roman captives he took, urging them to join his forces. But also he made clear to the Roman allies by frequent example the range of terror and devastation awaiting his enemies.

In Rome itself, there was not a word spoken of compromise or surrender. With Flaminius dead and the other consul isolated on the Adriatic coast, the Senate resorted to a measure which the Roman constitution provided for extreme emergencies. The people of the city were asked to elect a temporary dictator. The popular choice was an elderly aristocrat who had warned against the conflict with Carthage in the first place. His name was Quintus Fabius Maximus.

As a child Fabius was teased by his schoolmates for his slowness and docility. They called him "Ovicula"—"the Little Sheep." As a man Fabius was, above all, patient, unhurried, cautious. He considered each problem carefully, never rushing to the mistakes of judgment that plagued his more quick-witted colleagues. Like many patricians of the day Fabius took pride in rigid physical discipline and control; he was the master of his body, not its slave. Sensible, balanced, sane—but ruthlessly determined—Quintus Fabius Maximus was precisely the kind of man calculated to give the subtle, imaginative Hannibal the most trouble.

Fabius restored public confidence. He ordered a strict observance of all the old Roman religious ceremonies, many of them long forgotten. This united the citizens in an interlude of shared ritual. It diverted their minds from the recent defeats. It also shifted the blame for Rome's military setbacks from inept leadership to mere negligence in failing to satisfy the gods.

More practically, Fabius imposed heavy new taxes on

the Romans and their Latin allies. He demanded, too, a total effort to enlist fresh troops as replacements for the casualties of Trasimene.

Leaving veteran commanders behind to train the recruits, Fabius cautiously began to shadow the triumphant Carthaginian army. He located Hannibal moving south along the eastern coast, ravaging the Apulian countryside in a show of force. Instead of trying to halt the burning and looting, Fabius instructed the Roman allies to follow a "scorched-earth" policy. They were to burn their own crops, destroy their own houses, retreat to the protection of the walled cities.

Fabius wanted to avoid a pitched battle with his brilliant opponent. Rather, he would harass Hannibal, sting him with hit-and-run attacks, prevent him from feeding his army or getting reinforcements, keep him always off balance. Time, he reasoned, was on his side. Eventually Hannibal's army would be reduced to exhaustion and overwhelmed by the tide of Roman manpower.

Such tactics of withdrawal and harassment have ever since been known to history as "Fabian" tactics. They were notably successful against Hannibal, earning for the doggedly determined Roman general the title "Cunctator" ("the Delayer"). Such tactics, however, were risky. They could exasperate the impatient citizens and politicians of Rome.

Day after day Fabius and his men appeared on the distant ridges, the higher ground overlooking Hannibal's army. Occasionally they attacked a foraging party or ambushed a patrol. But Hannibal was unable to draw them into battle. Even when he ravaged fields before the very eyes of the Romans to torment them, they restrained their anger and avoided open combat. They would not be trapped.

Indeed, Fabius once turned the tables and hemmed in the Punic general. Marching westward in easy stages across the Apennines, Hannibal hoped to swerve northward to the strategic town of Casinum, thereby cutting a vital road. The city of Rome would be deprived of reinforcements and Fabius would find it difficult to avoid a general engagement.

Somehow, according to the historian Livy,* Hannibal's guide misunderstood him. It was a costly error. Instead of dominating the approaches to Rome from Casinum (site of the bloody battle between Allied and Nazi forces in World War II), Hannibal found himself at the little town of Caslinum—trapped in a blind ravine!

Fabius perceived the blunder at once. Quickly he stationed men on the heights overlooking both the entrance and the narrow exit to the valley. He was ready to attack. For once it appeared that Hannibal would have no way to escape.

In an uncharacteristic act of fury, the enraged Carthaginian leader ordered his guide flogged and then crucified. Disaster seemed imminent as darkness fell. Turning the problem over and over in his mind, Hannibal struck on an ingenious scheme.

While there was still daylight, he ordered his men to make torches of sticks and branches. These they bound to the horns of some 2,000 of the army's oxen. Later, toward midnight, he had his Spanish cattle herders, accustomed to hilly country, drive the animals up the slopes of the hills. At a signal the herders ignited the torches, and amid wild shouting, drove the beasts toward the Romans at the summit of the ridge.

The Romans, attracted by the sight of so many torches moving through the night, rushed to give battle. Their confusion was complete when the animals jostled in among them, along with a hail of javelins and stones thrown by the Spaniards. It was morning before the Romans disengaged themselves and regrouped. To their amazement they observed the last elements of the Carthaginian rear guard slipping through the deserted mountain pass below.

---

* For a contrasting view of this entire episode see the account of the Roman historian Polybius.

When the news of Hannibal's spectacular escape reached Rome, the enraged populace blamed Fabius. The city already was in turmoil. Plebeian orators crowded the rostrums, angrily denouncing Fabius as a coward for not meeting Hannibal in pitched battle. Food was in short supply because of the Punic leader's systematic devastation of the harvests, as well as Fabius' own scorched-earth policy. As grain prices rose the poverty-stricken plebeians suffered most. Moreover, the fury of the plebs was targeted on Fabius because his rich estate had been spared intentionally by the rampaging African armies.

Despite a vigorous campaign for reelection in the year 216, Fabius was defeated. His opponents scoffed at the aged leader's warnings that another victory for Hannibal could start a chain reaction of defections among the Italian allies.

"The war must be swiftly ended!" cried the smooth-talking plebeian candidate, M. Terrentius Varro. The devilish Carthaginians would be helpless, he argued, when confronted by the magnificent new Roman army now ready for action.

Varro was a man of little ability, but with a keen ear for the drift of public clamor. He was swept into office by his vociferous admirers. The patrician Consul elected for the year 216 was the elderly L. Aemilius Paulus, a member of the five-man delegation which originally had declared war on Carthage.

For six months the Romans prepared for battle—thoroughly, painstakingly, confidently. An army of eight legions was assembled, the greatest force in the history of the Republic. Slingers and archers poured in from Syracuse. More than 100 Senators volunteered for service. Wealthy merchants enlisted in the ranks. Impoverished farmers flocked to Rome, tempted by the prospect of acquiring slaves and rich booty when they crushed the Cathaginian army.

When word reached Rome that Hannibal had seized the fortress town of Cannae, ten miles from the Adriatic coast in Apulia, the impulsive Varro could no longer be restrained. He and his army, perhaps 87,000 strong, filed expectantly out of the gates of Rome. Behind them, wildly cheering townspeople were certain of impending victory.

At first everything went well for the Romans. An advance party of Roman legionaries reported in high elation that they had seized a Carthaginian camp—apparently deserted in such haste that the foe had left behind valuable inlaid weapons and table silver. Next, a band of Numidian cavalry was driven off with surprising ease. The confidence of the Roman troops soared; their thirst for combat increased. What was there to fear, they asked, from a one-eyed African with a tiny army?

According to Roman practice the two Consuls alternated command—one leading the legions one day, the other taking command the next day. On his day of command, Terrentius Varro raised the red flag above his tent—the order for general battle—over the protests of Aemilius Paulus.

It was the second day of August, 216 B.C., according to the Roman calendar. Actually, by our reckoning, it was some time in June.

Varro slowly began to move his troops across the Aufidus River to face the Carthaginians on the open plain of Cannae. Here, declared Varro with assurance, Hannibal could not resort to ambush; the brute strength and courage of the Roman infantry would crush him.

From a grassy knoll overlooking the plain, Hannibal and his staff officers shaded their eyes from the morning sun and watched the approach of the mighty legions. Thousands of soldiers formed into tight battle squares, wheeled, and then crossed the river. They outnumbered the

Carthaginians almost two to one. The procession seemed endless.

As the Punic officers, seated on their horses, watched, Gisco, a grizzled veteran of Hannibal's campaigns, whispered his astonishment at the sight of so many men.

"There is something even more astonishing, which you have not noticed," replied Hannibal, gazing without expression at the impressive parade of advancing Romans.

"What is that?" asked Gisco apprehensively, thinking of some unseen disaster.

"Among all of them," said Hannibal, "there is not one named Gisco."

The tension of the officers broke. Laughing and relaxed, they cantered down from the knoll to rejoin their units. Soon the story of Gisco spread through the ranks; the army unwound. Hannibal, like other great men, had a capacity for joking on the brink of an ordeal.

Hannibal's lightheartedness was not without reason. He must have watched with delight from his vantage point as the Romans formed their battle line. Varro packed his infantry tightly together in the center, clearly betraying his certainty that victory lay in smashing the Carthaginian middle—precisely the gambit Hannibal was counting on. One unit of Roman cavalry under Aemilius Paulus was posted on the right. But it was wedged so tightly between the river and the massed legions in the center that its maneuverability was limited. Varro himself commanded still other Roman horsemen on the left. Foolishly he had divided his cavalry, although this was the one area in which he was inferior to the Carthaginians.

Facing Aemilius, on the left wing of his army, Hannibal placed Spanish and African heavy cavalry under a trusted officer, Hasdrubal. On the right were his fast-riding Numidians, led by Hanno. But it was at the center that Hannibal's disposition was most unusual. Opposite the deeply massed Roman legions he positioned only a thin line of Gauls and Libyans. They were strung for a mile and a half in an elongated crescent, bulging out toward the powerful Roman center. At each end of the weak crescent, however, he fixed hardy African infantry clothed in Roman armor taken from the dead of Trasimene. Hannibal and Mago, his dashing young brother, personally commanded the center.

A wild charge by Hasdrubal's cavalry launched the battle. Penned in between the river and the moving infantry columns, the Romans nonetheless resisted fiercely, and the fighting for a short while was hard. Then the Carthaginians got the better of it. Some Romans, including Aemilius, managed to escape on foot and melt into the ranks of the adjoining infantry. Most were cut down on the spot. Hasdrubal took no prisoners; he had other things to do.

In a superb feat of horsemanship Hasdrubal next led his men the entire length of the field—behind the Roman lines. He linked with Maharbal, who was already closely engaged against Varro. After pausing for only a moment to regroup, his horsemen swept savagely down on the rear of the unsuspecting Romans, emitting primitive war cries and hurling their javelins as they rode.

Just then, with the field in confusion, 500 Numidian soldiers who had claimed to be defectors executed their part of the plan. They drew knives concealed under their shirts and began slashing and stabbing their captors. Between the panic they created and the fierce onslaught of Hasdrubal's cavalry, the Roman flank dissolved in chaos.

Maneuvering for fighting room, Varro's unit became separated from the battle. The decision at Cannae was still in doubt when the battle's instigator, M. Terrentius Varro, fled the scene, accompanied by only a handful of horsemen.

While the Roman flanks were crumbling, their powerful center delivered blow after blow to the thinly drawn Carthaginian middle. Fighting obstinately, the Spaniards and Gauls slowly fell back, directed masterfully by Hannibal himself. Step by step they withdrew toward higher ground. Like an elastic band their crescent bulge became a straight line, then an inverted funnel.

Into the breach poured the excited Romans, roaring their victory cry. Throwing caution to the winds, they ran forward. The carefully drawn battle square gradually transformed itself into a pointed wedge—locking itself into the funnel. Soon, only the men in the front ranks could wield their weapons; those behind merely pushed into each other. Legion after legion pressed into the gaping entryway Hannibal held open for them. And all the while the stolid African infantrymen stood firm at the hinges of the giant gates.

Tired, hungry, a steady wind blowing dust into their eyes, the sun blinding them, the Romans' predicament grew more serious by the minute. They were hopelessly packed together within the grasp of the Punic army.

Then, at precisely the right moment, Hannibal ordered the gates swung shut. At his signal the African infantry closed in, linked together, and completed the encirclement of the Romans.

At last recognizing their peril, the gallant legions struggled to break through the trap as they had before at the Ticinus and the Trebia. And they might have succeeded again since they still far outnumbered the Carthaginians. It was then, however, that Hannibal put into effect the final phase of his brilliant plan.

Executing his assignment perfectly, Hasdrubal broke off his pursuit of Varro's tattered force and stormed back onto the field. With full fury the Numidian cavalry struck the Roman rear. What resulted was not a battle but a massacre. With professional skill, the swift-moving horsemen herded the legionaries into small clusters. Then they simply slashed them to ribbons. Foot soldiers were helpless against such well-disciplined men on horseback.

Aemilius Paulus, although badly wounded, refused to leave his comrades. He fell under a shower of javelins.

By late afternoon the slaughter was complete. Fugitive bands of Roman survivors fled to the fortress town of Canusium. Some wandered from the scene alone, dazed and stupefied. The splendid army that had filed out of Rome with such high confidence was no more.

That evening, on horseback, Hannibal picked his way across the grizzly battlefield. Bodies of friend and foe alike lay in his path. Everywhere he was greeted by his men with shouts and cheers. Admiring officers, still astonished by the incredible victory, offered him their congratulations. He refused to rest, as they asked him to do. His first concern was arranging medical care for the wounded and a hearty meal, with wine, for his weary men.

The brave Carthaginian officer, Maharbal, exhilarated by the victory, implored his chief not to stop there.

"Within five days you shall hold a conqueror's feast in Rome," declared the rugged warrior. "Pursue them. I will go before you with my cavalry, and they shall know you have come before they know you are coming."

"I thank you for your zeal, Maharbal," answered Hannibal, "but I must have time to think about it."

The fierce Carthaginian angrily responded, in words the truth of which historians debate even today:

"The gods do not give all their gifts to one man, Hannibal. You know how to conquer, not how to use a conquest!"

Without reply the great general rode off to care for his men and to rest for the night among the sentries.

A blanket of cold darkness descended on the bloody plain of Cannae. August 2, 216 B.C., was over.

# CHAPTER 6

# THE
# PUNIC TIDE
# EBBS

The first slanting rays of morning sunlight revealed the holocaust in all its starkness. It was a scene, says Livy, "at which even our enemies must have shuddered":

> Many thousands of the Roman dead lay there,
> foot soldiers and horsemen as chance had
> thrown them together. . . . Some were cut
> down as they rose covered with blood from
> the field of death, revived by the cold of
> the morning which had closed their wounds.
> Some who were discovered still alive, with
> their thigh tendons cut, bared their throats
> and begged the foe to shed what blood remained
> in them. Others were found with their heads
> buried in holes . . . they had suffocated
> themselves.

Of the superb Roman army, numbering approximately 87,000 men, more than 60,000 were killed, 7,000 captured. Some historians place the number of dead as high as 70,000 —close to the magnitude of casualties inflicted in modern

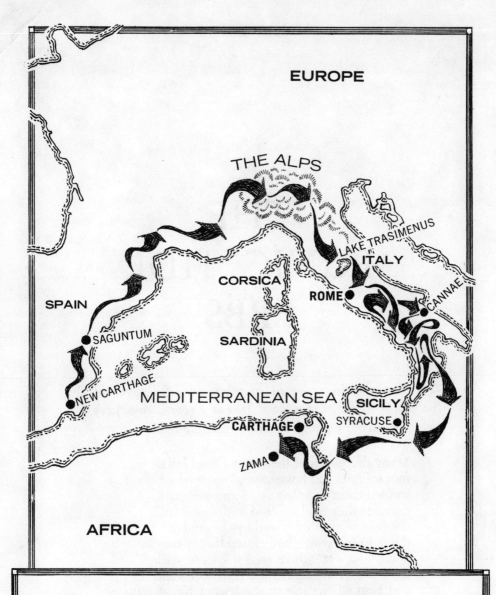

EUROPE

THE ALPS

SPAIN

CORSICA

LAKE TRASIMENUS

ITALY

ROME

CANNAE

SAGUNTUM

SARDINIA

NEW CARTHAGE

MEDITERRANEAN SEA

SICILY

SYRACUSE

CARTHAGE

ZAMA

AFRICA

# Hannibal's Route
## in His Campaign Against the Romans

 LINE OF MARCH

warfare when an atomic bomb was dropped on Hiroshima, Japan, in 1945, at the conclusion of World War II.

The Consul, Aemilius Paulus, eighty senators, and twenty-nine military tribunes perished on the field of Cannae. The Carthaginian loss was under 6,000 men, two-thirds of them Gauls. Remarkably, all of this carnage took place in an area about the size of Central Park in New York City.

Never again would the Romans—or any other major power—rely so heavily on infantry. And not for the next 2,000 years could the lesson of Cannae be neglected by military tacticians.

"The Romans," said Polybius, their perceptive historian, "were most to be feared when they stood in real danger." The weeks following the disaster at Cannae were such a time; they marked the supreme test of the Republic. In Livy's words, "Rome had no camp, no general, no soldiers." Hannibal was master of nearly the whole of Italy. Carthage had surrendered under much less calamitous circumstances in the First Punic War. It is to the everlasting credit of the Roman people that in their time of greatest peril they neither despaired of victory nor lost their nerve. Unlike Carthage, they had no shortsighted peace party.

As news of the catastrophe at Cannae fell upon the stunned populace of the great city, one man had the strength to assert himself—the staunch old patrician, Quintus Fabius Maximus.

Soft-spoken and patient, Fabius could also be ruthlessly determined. He brooked no criticism of his authority. Without hesitation he took over all the powers of a dictator.

Fabius moved first of all to end the bewilderment and stem the tide of panic. He had scouts sent out to collect accurate information on Hannibal's whereabouts. Next he ordered the women, who had been shrilly lamenting the dead, confined to their homes and insisted that silence be maintained in the city. He hastily mustered a force of old men and young boys to man the fortifications. No one was permitted to leave the city limits. The Senate adjourned. The Forum was cleared.

As he had after Trasimene, Fabius turned to religious ritual to calm the people. He ordered a barbaric sacrifice to the gods: a Greek man and woman and a Gallic man and woman were buried alive in a walled pit where these primitive rites had been conducted in times of trouble long past. The Romans, then a simple, superstitious people, were awed by the solemnity of the occasion. Gradually, they calmed themselves. Order was restored.

With grim tenacity the Republic stood firm. The shrewd Carthaginian commander, Carthalo, dispatched by Hannibal as a peace envoy, was denied entry to the city. The lictor sent to meet him in the Alban Hills declared that he would speak not a word of peace; Carthalo was given until sunset to leave Roman territory. Then, for fear that money would help Hannibal's cause, the Senate refused to ransom the Roman prisoners taken at Cannae, although the Senators knew full well that the men would certainly be sold into slavery. Other soldiers who fled the battle were sentenced to a long term of humiliating service in Sicily. The Roman code of warfare allowed few exceptions to the doctrine of "conquer or die." Significantly, Varro, who had fled the battle but courageously rallied many of the survivors, was welcomed back to the city and thanked "for not despairing of the Republic." He still had an influential popular following.

Faced with disaster, the Romans mounted a massive war effort. Class divisions that had split the state were temporarily forgotten; all classes and parties agreed to the supreme power of the Senate. Wealthy families contributed slaves to the new army that was being formed and advanced money for weapons on only a promise of later payment. The temples were stripped of their war trophies to speed the process of rearmament. The allies agreed to a double rate of tribute—voluntarily. Roman military units overseas were informed that no pay would be forthcoming; they would have to fend for themselves. Meanwhile, by accepting young boys as recruits, along with criminals, debtors, and more than 8,000 slaves, four new legions were pieced together.

For a month the city stood poised, waiting for Hannibal to unleash a hammer blow. It never came.

Hannibal earnestly desired peace after Cannae. He regarded a direct assault on Rome as impractical. Even if he took the city, he might not be able to hold it against the onslaught of Roman reinforcements. He might find himself in serious tactical difficulty. Furthermore, if there were no peace, he would be obliged to woo the loyal Roman allies, not a simple task. Finally, as Fabius wisely predicted, time was on the side of Rome; even the extraordinary casualties of Cannae probably could be replaced.

Consequently, when the Roman lictor spurned Carthalo's offer to negotiate, Hannibal knew, if his soldiers did not, that a long and bitter struggle lay ahead.

At first, Hannibal's triumph at Cannae greatly improved his prospects. The sale of unransomed Roman prisoners in the slave market at Delos filled his campaign chest with silver. Booty gleaned from the field of battle was mountainous—jewelry, weapons, shields, armor.

Even the Carthaginian homeland responded this time. Hannibal's brother Mago could do more than just plead for some slight help. He dramatically poured out on a table in front of the wide-eyed elders of the Council the contents of a basket. In it were 6,000 gold seal rings taken from the fingers of slaughtered Roman nobles at Cannae. For once the ungrateful Carthaginians agreed, if reluctantly, to reinforce their generals in the field.

Four thousand Numidian horsemen and a few elephants were assigned to Hannibal, while a somewhat larger levy of recruits was sent to his brother Hasdrubal, still fighting in Spain. The choice was significant, showing clearly that the Punic legislators valued the site of their silver mines in

Spain more highly than the fate of their nation which was being decided in Italy.

Hannibal's most important dividends from Cannae were political. In rapid succession, the peoples of southern Italy renounced their loyalty to Rome and sided with him. The Lucanians, the Bruttians, the Apulians, and the warlike Samnites all cast their lot with Carthage. Skillfully Hannibal catered to their sympathies, guaranteeing them protection from Rome, promising them release from the heavy tribute they annually had been required to pay.

Support came from key centers. The old Greek colony of Capua, always envious of Rome and hopeful of displacing it as the leading city in Italy, enthusiastically declared for Carthage. And even overseas, Philip V of Macedon, heir to the legend of Alexander the Great, concluded an alliance with Hannibal and declared war on Rome. Then, moving adroitly, Hannibal arranged an internal revolt that brought the vital Sicilian city of Syracuse into his camp.

Only Umbria, Latium, and Etruria—Rome's neighbors in central Italy—remained loyal; all the others flocked to join the African invader. Hannibal, fighting virtually alone before the battle of Cannae, was now the leader of a coalition spearheaded by Carthage, Macedon, and Syracuse—unlikely allies united only in their determination to check the advance of Roman power.

Content that his years of campaigning were at last bearing fruit, Hannibal led his army into winter quarters at Capua.

No city in Italy was more blessed with abundance than Capua. Twelve miles north of Naples, its winters were balmy, its style of living easy and open. Always a pearl in the Greek overseas empire, Greek culture and learning still flourished there. For the winter of 216–15 weary veterans of Hannibal's punishing Alpine crossing and his four pitched battles against the Roman war machine luxuriated in Capuan hospitality. They were welcomed not as conquerors but as guests.

Day after day the soldiers feasted and indulged themselves in the pleasures of an extravagant city. With plenty of silver in their pockets, they could well afford to pay for delicious wine and the company of the beautiful women of southern Italy. Slaves were at their beck and call.

It was to be an unforgettable winter for Hannibal's men. Some argue that because of it the Carthaginian army never again recovered the discipline, the fighting edge that carried them to their early victories. "Capua," says Livy, "was Hannibal's Cannae."

Probably more destructive to the Cathaginian spirit than the delights of Capua were the new tactics adopted by the Roman armies. Taught a fearful lesson by Hannibal's memorable triumphs, they now fully implemented the advice of Quintus Fabius Maximus. For the next several years Fabius personally directed the war against Hannibal.

Cautiously, painstakingly, Fabius stalked his foe. Year after year the Roman legions grew stronger, their numbers increasing as the Carthaginian ranks thinned. Fabius, the Delayer, became a great general because he would not fight. When Hannibal's veterans fell in battle, they were usually replaced by less-reliable, less-committed troops. And although none of the magic disappeared from the great Punic leader's moves—always imaginative, unexpected, slashing—he became imprisoned, as it were, in the land of his conquests. The Roman navy controlled the seas, preventing aid from reaching him; Fabius tormented him, delivering annoying little jabs at his patrols, sapping his strength little by little.

Much of the story of the years following Cannae is told in Hannibal's marches and countermarches, often futile, across southern Italy. Fabius would not be drawn into battle. Meanwhile, Roman numerical superiority began to grow.

The first major crack in the Hannibalic alliance system came with Rome's recapture of Syracuse in 211 B.C. For two years the legendary center of Greek culture on Sicily was besieged by the Consul Marcellus. He tried first to take it by storming the sea wall. But ingenious defenses, personally designed during the siege by the great astronomer and mathematician Archimedes, baffled him. Great catapults fired missiles far out to sea; shorter-range artillery dropped lead balls the size of sheep through the wooden hulls of Marcellus' warships; huge clawlike cranes lifted smaller craft completely out of the water and then released them to their destruction. An assault by land also failed, stymied by other war engines of Archimedes' invention.

Marcellus, exhibiting characteristic Roman tenacity, kept trying. He blockaded the city and took steps to starve it into submission. This, too, failed.

Finally, one night when the celebration of a feast drew some of the sentries from their posts, the Romans scaled the walls. An informer had betrayed the city. Exasperated by the long siege, Marcellus broke promises made previously to the Syracusans and gave his troops free rein to loot. In the general confusion that followed, a party of Roman soldiers came upon the seventy-five-year-old Archimedes working on a mathematical problem in his chamber. There was a brief argument. With little time to waste on an old man, the soldiers ran the great scientist through with their swords and went back to their plundering.

Stripped of its great treasury, its works of art and statuary, Syracuse would never again recapture its former glory. It has since remained a secondary provincial town.

Hannibal, encamped at Tarentum in the heel of the Italian boot, was stunned to learn of the city's fall. But he had scarcely digested the news when an even more ominous report arrived. Capua—his principal base of operations in Italy—was under siege! If he did not relieve it immediately, it would be overwhelmed.

When Hannibal arrived at Capua, he found the Romans firmly entrenched around the city. Probing at their defenses, he was driven back. Breaking the siege, he concluded, would cost massive casualties.

Instead he decided on an indirect move—one of dazzling proportions. Assembling his troops and animals overnight, he struck out the next morning in quick march toward Rome itself. Along the way he paused to burn crops and spread terror, hoping to advertise his march and draw the besieging army away from Capua.

The scheme almost worked. Panic once again gripped the citizens of Rome. Aged Senators were called upon to rejoin their military units. The blood-curdling war cry of Hannibal's African horsemen sent refugees pouring into the capital city. Finally, Hannibal himself arrived at the Collina Gate, entry point to Rome on the northwest. Behind him, he left a ring of burning suburban villages; smoke from the fires billowed skyward within easy view from the Forum.

Accompanied by his staff officers the great Carthaginian warrior conducted a leisurely inspection tour on horseback, examining the city's defenses, pointing out places of interest. No record remains of his thoughts as he beheld the city whose power he had labored to crush for so many years. A schoolboy story has it that he cast a spear at one of the gates. But the tale may be dismissed; Hannibal was not the man to indulge in petulant gestures.

For several days Hannibal's forces ravaged the surrounding countryside. They replenished their treasury with rich stores of silver and gold, and with precious ornaments from sacred temples in the Alban Hills.

Inside the city walls, old Quintus Fabius Maximus stood firm in the face of public clamor that he call for reinforcements. He correctly diagnosed Hannibal's real aim to be the diversion of Roman forces from Capua. This time luck was on the side of Fabius. The Punic army arrived only a few days after two fully equipped legions had gathered in Rome from outlying towns for their annual training exercises. These provided just the extra cushion of protection that Fabius needed.

Hannibal realized unhappily that to assault the walled city would be futile. Still, he paused long enough for a joke.

Following a blare of trumpets, he sent a single messenger to the city gates with a wry Carthaginian business proposition: after Hannibal's victories the shops in the Roman Forum would be put up for sale anyway; what was he bid for them in advance? The Romans, never renowned for their sense of humor, did not answer.

Hannibal soon vanished with his army into the countryside, convinced that his feint had drawn enough troops from Capua to lift the siege. He was well along on a lightning march southward when disastrous news reached him. Capua had fallen to the Romans! Its leaders had been beheaded; its surviving citizens either exiled or sold into slavery for befriending Carthage.

With no further need for speed, Hannibal angrily turned on the Roman force pursuing him and slashed it to pieces. Then, cleverly eluding the enemy force operating from his former base at Capua, he swiftly marched to the toe of the boot in hopes of surprising the fortress town of Rhegium. Unable to take it, he retreated to his lair at Tarentum.

Yet, serious as the situation was, all was not lost. Hannibal still moved at will through all of southern Italy. He masterfully brushed aside or crushed any forces in his path. Meanwhile, the Roman economy was strained to exhaustion, a predicament aggravated by the destruction wrought by Hannibal around the capital city. The allied towns in Latium could no longer pay tribute; they had nothing left to give. All precious metals in Rome were confiscated; no woman could keep more than one ring for herself. Even in the chambers of the Roman Senate cries of "Stop the war!" were raised.

Hannibal had still another trump card to play. His brother Hasdrubal commanded a large army in Spain. If Hasdrubal could link hands with him by crossing the Alps into Italy, the combined Carthaginian army might prove too much for Rome. Together, the two might yet win the victory that Rome had denied to Hannibal alone.

# CHAPTER 7

# SCIPIO

Four more years passed with still more skirmishing, more marches and countermarches. But except for the recapture of Tarentum by Rome, the situation remained essentially unchanged. Early in the year 207 B.C. Hannibal had written to his brother Hasdrubal in Spain, urgently requesting aid. Otherwise, he said, the war in Italy could never be won. But communications were impossible. Months went by with no word. Hannibal knew that his brother had crossed the Alps, but beyond that fact he knew nothing.

Then, one day in late summer, a Roman horseman galloped audaciously up to the Carthaginian camp. Without pausing, he hurled a round object skyward, easily clearing the low-lying ramparts. The object was taken at once to Hannibal. It was the head of Hasdrubal.

The events preceding that ghastly incident hinged largely on chance. After crossing the Alps without opposition, Hasdrubal had struck southward out of the Po valley along the Adriatic coast. Hannibal had moved northward to join him. But between the sons of Hamilcar were ranged two Roman armies, one facing each brother. Hannibal had no more than 30,000 men, nearly two-thirds of them recently enlisted from among halfhearted allies in the Roman province of Bruttium. He could not force his way through the Roman lines to join his brother. Moreover, his network of spies had failed him. He did not know which road Hasdrubal was taking. Rather than risk the remnants of his army, he camped and waited for a message.

At this point a remarkable stroke of fortune played into the hands of the Roman Consul, Gaius Claudius Nero. Hasdrubal's messengers, four Gauls and two Numidians, fell into the hands of Roman foragers near Tarentum. Nero recognized at once the importance of the dispatch they carried. For a brief time he would know what both Carthaginian generals were doing, while they would be groping blindly for each other.

In a desperate, perhaps foolhardy gamble, he set out from the Aufidus River, not far from Cannae, to intercept Hasdrubal. Facing Hannibal, he left only a moderate force and numerous burning campfires.

Hasdrubal recognized the danger and tried to avoid a pitched battle. He hoped to slip away to the south on the Via Flaminia. But in another unforseen accident his guides lost their way in the darkness. Chance changed the course of the war. Hasdrubal was cornered at the Metaurus River and forced to fight a decisive battle. Although outnumbered, the gallant Carthaginian appeared to be winning when Nero took still another desperate gamble.

He detached a large unit of legionaries from his own right flank, leaving it completely exposed. Then, racing with these troops behind the entire length of his line, he struck in full force on the Carthaginian right. It crumbled, and the Romans rushed through the breach. In a vain attempt to rally his troops, Hasdrubal dashed into the midst of the carnage. He was struck down immediately.

The Romans then placed the head of the fallen commander on a pike and paraded it—before casting it brutally into Hannibal's camp.

The battle of the Metaurus was crucial. On its eve, Rome neared exhaustion, and a genuine peace movement was developing in the city. If the two Carthaginian armies had linked together, there is no telling what might have followed. Instead, Hannibal now retired to the mountain fastness of Bruttium. Although the Romans still respected the legend of his name and refused to do battle with him, Italy was no longer in danger. No Punic land army remained to provide him with reinforcements; Roman warships controlled the seas. Hannibal's position in Italy was hopeless.

When news of the battle at the Metaurus River reached Rome, the citizens exploded in hysterical celebration, so great had been their anxiety and apprehension.

There now entered upon the scene one of the extraordinary personalities of the ancient world—Publius Cornelius Scipio. His father was the Publius Cornelius Scipio whom Hannibal eluded to cross the Alps and enter Italy. Young Publius had fought at the Trebia. He had saved his father's life at the Ticinus. Then, at the age of eighteen, he had survived the slaughter at Cannae.

After the Cannae disaster, Livy relates, certain Roman nobles, led by Caecilius Metellus, were planning to leave Italy and enter the service of some foreign king. Gathering a few followers, young Scipio burst in on a meeting of the nobles. He drew his sword over the head of Metellus. Then he repeated his own oath of allegiance: "I solemnly swear that I will not abandon the Roman Republic, nor permit any other Roman citizen to do so; and if I knowingly break this oath, oh, Jupiter Optimus Maximus, visit me, my house, my kinsmen, my estate with utter destruction."

Scipio demanded that Metellus and all the others take the same oath. "Whoever will not swear it," he said, "let him know that this sword is drawn against him."

Ashamed, cowed, and more than a little inspired, they all took the oath and agreed to follow Scipio.

Scarcely more than an adolescent, Scipio had supreme confidence in himself and almost mystical power over others. He was sensitive, imaginative—a bit of a dreamer. Around the bathhouses of Rome it was whispered that he would sometimes meditate alone through entire nights in the Temple of Jupiter on the Capitoline Hill.

Why did he behave so strangely? Perhaps, concluded the superstitious, unsophisticated Romans more than two centuries before Jesus, the rumors really were true—Publius Cornelius Scipio was actually the earthly son of Jupiter himself! In later years his soldiers would swear that their commander performed miracles: caused waters to halt so they might pass, foretold the moves of the enemy. With subtlety uncommon for a Roman, though not unlike the Carthaginian Hannibal, Scipio played on mass superstition and created an image of himself as invincible and supernatural.

Romans remembered his heroism at Cannae, where there were all too few Roman heroes. They half-believed that he communed with unseen gods. Also, his family was one of the most distinguished and influential in Rome. It is not surprising then, that in 210 B.C. the Senate unanimously bestowed upon him the proconsulship in Spain, although, at age twenty-four, he was not legally old enough to be even a praetor.

Ramrod thin and handsome, coldly intelligent, but possessed of great charm and diplomatic skill, Scipio (like Caesar) was passionately ambitious. He viewed the command in Spain as a steppingstone to greater things.

But ambition never blinded him to strategic realities. He painstakingly studied the tactics of Hannibal, learned from him, even, it is said, copied the great Carthaginian's smile and mannerisms. Almost alone among the Romans, Scipio realized that the true enemy of his country was not Hannibal but Carthage. Without Carthage, he argued, Hannibal would be helpless in Italy. Therefore his long-range objective was to crush Carthage itself.

Five years before Scipio the Younger was elected to the proconsulship in Spain, his father had recovered from the wounds he suffered at the Trebia and returned to the Iberian

theater of operations. Scipio the Elder was strikingly successful, especially in his campaigns on the Spanish coast. In order
to halt him and protect their silver mines, the Carthaginian
Council diverted to Spain reserve forces which otherwise
would have reached Hannibal in Italy. Fighting alongside
Hannibal, those reinforcements might have proved decisive.

Over several years, Scipio the Elder and his brother,
Gnaeus, extended their activities and even threatened the
vital Punic base at New Carthage. But, outnumbered, their
supply lines strung too thinly, they became vulnerable. In
the spring of 211 B.C., Hasdrubal caught them away from
their base. Both Roman generals were killed, their armies
badly decimated.

After his election by the Senate as proconsul, Publius
Cornelius Scipio the Younger, wasted little time in avenging
his father's death at the hands of Hasdrubal. In 209 he
audaciously swept down on the garrison at Carthagena; he
caught it completely by surprise. Here was a stroke reminis-
cent of Hannibal's lightning raids in Italy. Scipio had learned
his lessons well. With one roundhouse punch he deprived
Carthage of its principal source of silver and established a
base for further advances into Andalusia.

But Scipio, shrewdly realistic, knew he was not yet
ready to challenge the Carthaginians in open battle. There
was careful groundwork to be laid first. Few commanders
were as adept at handling the myriad of details that win
battles as was Scipio.

Like Hannibal, he used his great charm to court the
friendship of the Spanish chieftains—cajoling them, sooth-
ing their pride, flattering them. Like Hannibal, too, he released all hostages to their own tribes. Meanwhile, he armed
his men with superb Spanish swords and drilled them relent-
lessly in his own adaptation of Punic military tactics. For
some of his troops the rehearsals proved more rigorous than
the battles.

In 208 Scipio advanced to Baecula in southern Spain. There he met Hasdrubal. Scipio's attempt to use an enveloping movement, as Hannibal had at Cannae, failed primarily because of inadequate cavalry strength. Hasdrubal cleverly withdrew the center of his line from the trap and escaped. The quick-thinking Carthaginian then disengaged altogether, preserving his army intact. He swiftly turned to the east and marched toward the Alps.

Scipio did not pursue him. Instead he turned back to Spain to secure the almost certain triumph of Roman arms there.

It was 206 B.C. before Scipio again lured the Carthaginians into a set fight. At the Battle of Ilipa, near modern Seville, Scipio destroyed the enemy's flanks, then methodically mopped up the remnants of the Punic center. He did the job with all the thoroughness Hannibal had displayed at Cannae.

Ilipa was the decisive battle of the Spanish war. It enabled Scipio to drive the disorganized armies of Mago, Hannibal's only surviving brother, back to the gates of Gades (modern Cadiz). Soon, Gades surrendered. Founded by Phoenician merchants perhaps as early as 900 B.C.—some 250 years before Carthage itself—Gades was the first overseas base of the Carthaginian empire. With its capture, Punic power in Spain collapsed. By 205 B.C. Spain was a Roman province.

Scipio wasted little time organizing his conquests. He was a young man in a hurry—impatient perhaps for glory, perhaps for an end to Rome's agony. Whatever he was looking for, it could come in only one way—victory in a direct confrontation with the peerless Hannibal.

# CHAPTER 8

# SCIPIO *VERSUS* HANNIBAL

The initiative in the war had passed from Carthage to Rome. No longer could Hannibal reasonably expect to conquer Italy. But the exhausted Romans could not follow up their victory at the Metaurus and destroy Hannibal.

Scipio was certain he had the answer. His plan was bold and risky. It was a total departure from the static, defensive strategy Rome had followed throughout the Hannibalic War. He would strike directly across the Mediterranean against Carthage, thereby forcing Hannibal to leave Italy and defend his homeland.

Quietly, Scipio began to move. After seizing Gades, he crossed the straits into Africa with only a small personal escort. He bore a safe-conduct pass signed by—of all people —Syphax, King of Numidia—Carthage's closest ally!

Scipio knew that for victory in Africa he needed excellent horsemen. And since the first clash at the Ticinus with Scipio's father, Hannibal had demonstrated that no cavalry in the Mediterranean world could compare with the remarkable Numidians. What would happen, reasoned Scipio, if Numidia's allegiance were to Rome instead of Carthage? If the Numidians had sold their services to one side, might they not sell them to the other—provided the price was right?

Syphax was guardedly receptive. At his lavish home near the now-forgotten town of Siga, the crafty desert chieftain prepared a sumptuous dinner for Scipio. For both men the stakes were high; no expense was spared. But to the Roman general's astonishment another guest appeared at the dinner: a noble Carthaginian named Hasdrubal (not related to Hannibal), who had been Mago's co-commander at Ilipa.

Needless to say, it was an unusual dinner party. Though Syphax was the charming host, neither of his guests trusted each other or him.

Scipio left Siga with a warm promise of alliance from the smooth-tongued Syphax. He strongly suspected, however, that Hasdrubal had departed with a promise of Numidia's continued friendship for Carthage. Syphax would wait as long as possible, determined to cast his lot with the stronger power.

A more convincing pledge came out of Scipio's negotiations with one Masinissa, the colorful chieftain of a tiny principality in eastern Numidia. Masinissa hated Syphax and craved to unite all of Numidia under his own leadership. He appears also to have fallen under the spell of Scipio's magnetic personality. If a Roman army landed in Africa, declared Masinissa, he would support it with a sizable body of well-trained horsemen.

With these diplomatic preliminaries behind him, Scipio had only to win over the Roman Senate to his plan for an invasion of Africa.

The last reserve funds had been taken from their secret hiding place in the Roman treasury. The Latin allies had been unable to pay their share of tribute for the past five years. The high odds that such an expedition aimed at the mighty walls of Carthage might fail loomed large in the Senate's deliberations.

Meanwhile, behind the scenes, Scipio's opponents, led by the aged hero, Quintus Fabius Maximus, whispered the real reason for their opposition to the expedition. They feared Scipio almost as much as they feared Hannibal. They were convinced that his real intention was to destroy the constitution and make himself Dictator of Rome.

In the consular elections of 205 Scipio won in a landslide. The Senate *had* to listen to such a popular leader. But it authorized only thirty ships for his use and only those legions which had been exiled to Sicily in disgrace after Cannae. Whatever volunteers he could attract and whatever additional costs he incurred were to be his own affair. The terms of the commission were close to humiliating.

Scipio accepted.

Anticipating the Roman invasion of Africa, the Carthaginian government responded on several fronts. It reinforced Hannibal's holding action in Bruttium and Lucania, where he managed to keep the Romans pinned against him. It dispatched his brother Mago to northern Italy by sea to spur the Gallic tribes into activity. And it raised a new army in the Carthaginian back country.

Discouraging news arrived in Carthage at this time. Philip V of Macedon had defected from the alliance system and made peace with Rome. Now the Roman legions long preoccupied in Illyria could be freed for service in Africa. But the loss was offset by Syphax's decision to cast his lot irrevocably with Carthage. Scipio had been right in his suspicions after the memorable dinner at Siga; he could not count on Syphax's help. In a letter to young Scipio, the African chieftain warned the Roman leader: "Do not invade Africa!"

P. Cornelius Scipio was not accustomed to heeding the warnings of petty desert princelings. In the spring of 204 B.C. an invasion fleet set sail under his command. It landed at Utica, a city engaged in bitter commercial rivalry with Carthage, located only twenty miles from the walls of the Punic capital.

Unexpectedly, Utica resisted Scipio. He was driven back with heavy losses and forced to settle into a time-consuming siege. Meanwhile, the noble Hasdrubal had strengthened his alliance with Syphax (first arranged at the memorable Siga dinner). He did this by giving in marriage to the aged Numidian chieftain his beautiful young daughter, Sophonisba. Beguiling, intelligent, thoroughly schooled in Greek culture, Sophonisba encouraged Syphax to superhuman efforts on behalf of Carthage. He raised a great army to oppose Scipio. By contrast, Masinissa, for all his promises, greeted the Roman expeditionary force with only 200 horsemen.

Scipio was not to be denied, however. The next spring he broke an armistice with Hasdrubal and Syphax in a deceitful pre-dawn surprise attack on their camp. The two African leaders barely escaped with their lives. Following up his advantage, Scipio destroyed the bulk of the Carthaginian army in the Battle of the Great Plains. Masinissa, heavily reinforced, mopped up the remnants of Syphax's forces and proudly displayed his long-time foe in chains before his cheering armies. He then occupied the Numidian Royal Palace.

At the palace gates Sophonisba pleaded with the handsome young cavalryman not to turn her over to the Romans. So lovely, so helpless was she that Masinissa developed an uncontrollable passion for her.

The affair continued until Scipio himself had to intervene. Claiming that Sophonisba was a Carthaginian agent and a captive of the Roman state, he demanded her surrender.

Though Masinissa was emotional and romantic, he was still a sensible man. One night he entered the chamber of the ravishing enchantress—a goblet of poisoned wine in his hand. Either she must return to Rome with Syphax, or take the poison.

Thanking her lover for such an unusual bridal gift, she

calmly drank the wine and died. The Romans lost no time in installing Masinissa as King of Greater and Lesser Numidia—an area comprising parts of modern Libya and Algeria. They presented him with a golden crown and an ivory scepter. He became the first, but by no means the last, of the puppet kings in Rome's expanding overseas empire.

Scipio was not yet ready to complete the conquest of Carthage. He needed time to reorganize his armies, time to plan his next moves. Behind the triple walls that protected the Punic capital, the Council and the Shofets also decided they needed time—at least long enough for Hannibal to race to their rescue. The Carthaginian elders accepted the peace treaty offered to them by Scipio, intending never to honor its terms. An armistice was arranged.

Secretly, the Council placed Hanno, the aging cavalry hero of Cannae, in command of the city's defenses. It sent urgent messages to Hannibal and Mago to return to Carthage.

Mago never arrived. He died on shipboard of wounds suffered in his final battle in northern Italy and was buried at sea. So perished Hannibal's last brother, a leader helpful to Hannibal in his plans and battles but always in his shadow.

Only Hannibal himself now remained to carry on his father's struggle against Rome. Before leaving Bruttium, the Punic wizard took time for a final jest. Since crossing the Alps, he had seen countless monuments and tablets raised by the pretentious Romans to their accomplishments and honors. So, overlooking the sea near the port of Croton, Hannibal erected his own bronze memento—a simple tablet listing his long string of triumphs over the Latin armies during fifteen years on the Italian peninsula.

Characteristically, he then slipped unnoticed out of Croton. Most of his men were carried in sixty captured Roman transport ships; the rest in ships provided by the Carthaginian Council, finally fearful of Carthage's own safety. Two weeks later, to the consternation of Scipio, Hannibal landed—four days' march to the east of Carthage—with his army intact. He had eluded the entire Roman naval squadron sent to intercept him.

In Rome, Hannibal's departure was marked by five days of official thanksgiving. In Carthage, his arrival was greeted with sighs of relief.

And what of Hannibal? After thirty-six years, he was once again on African soil. Half-blind, his brothers dead, his victories in Italy all for nothing, what must he have thought as he watched the surviving veterans of his years of campaigning file down the gangplanks of ships and pass him in review?

Events pressed in on him, leaving little time for nostalgia. Shortly after his arrival, the Carthaginian Council declared the armistice ended. Hannibal was already gathering an army. At its core was the army of Italy—remnants of the proud striking force which he had first led across the Alps. There were fewer Spaniards and Africans now, but a host of Lucanians, Bruttians, Gauls, and Roman deserters. Mago's army, without their leader, had crossed safely into Africa and joined Hannibal. The sons of Syphax contributed a contingent of cavalry. Carthage itself raised an infantry force. There were eighty fine war elephants.

When Hannibal learned that Masinissa's vital cavalry was still engaged in conquering the towns of Syphax's old kingdom, leaving Scipio vulnerable, he did not hesitate. He gave orders to his army to move out at once. The battle for Africa, indeed the battle for control of the entire Mediterranean basin, was fast approaching a climax.

It was spring of the year 202 B.C. Hannibal cut across the Roman line of march and encamped near a little town less than fifty miles south of Carthage.

The name of the town was Zama.

Scipio expected Hannibal to strike by surprise. He was

perplexed, therefore, when an envoy from the mighty Carthaginian appeared in his camp. Hannibal wished to meet him personally. The Roman Consul agreed. Uneasily he scanned the horizon, hoping that Masinissa would return. A little later he was rewarded as the flamboyant desert bandit thundered into view at the head of 6,000 wild-riding Numidian horsemen. Now the Romans were clearly superior in cavalry—the all important factor on an open plain such as Zama presented.

Secure in the knowledge that he would not be the victim of another Cannae for want of horses, Scipio proceeded to his historic appointment with Hannibal.

They met on a barren wasteland separating the two armies. Each general left his lines with a small escort and rode for a short distance into the plain. Then, dismounting, they approached each other on foot, accompanied only by their interpreters.

For a long time they stood face to face, absolutely still. Neither spoke; neither flinched. Here were the two greatest warriors of their time. Hannibal, the grizzled African hero, now forty-five years old but still strong and confident, gazed with almost fatherly interest at the lean young patrician opposite him. Scipio, bareheaded, handsome, somewhat shorter than his foe, waited tensely, every nerve alerted. He showed no emotion as he returned Hannibal's look directly. Yet only with difficulty could the brilliant Latin conceal his admiration for this subtle older man whose every move on the battlefield he had committed to memory. What eternities must have passed through the minds of these two before Hannibal broke the silence.

With courtesy and high dignity the Punic leader addressed his young adversary. Through the official accounts of Polybius and Livy we know in bare outline what was said: Hannibal spoke of his regret that the two great empires had ever encroached on each other's spheres. He pointed out that it was not yet too late to make peace. He told of his respect for Scipio's father, with whom he had fought the opening engagements of the great war. Would it not be well, he asked Scipio, to seek an end to the killing? Did he think the fortunes of war might not again turn, as they had turned against Carthage following Cannae?

Scipio listened. Then quietly he asked Hannibal for his terms.

Carthage would acknowledge the loss of Spain, Hannibal responded, and also the islands of the sea between Africa and Italy. But it would not return Roman fugitives and deserters, now an integral part of the Punic army. This requirement of the recently broken peace treaty could not be honored.

Scipio was in no position, he said, to accept less than the Senate already had agreed upon. There could be no more concessions made to Carthage than the treaty permitted.

The two spoke of other matters at length, possibly things they chose never to reveal. Then they turned and rejoined their escorts. For the present, nothing more could be settled by words.

The next morning at first light, the contending armies aligned themselves on the plain of Zama. Hannibal's force was slightly larger but not as well trained. As always, it was composed of warriors of many races, but this time of men who never before had fought together. The eighty Carthaginian elephants, too, were young and unaccustomed to combat. Scipio's Numidian cavalry gave him a decided advantage.

To counter the strength of Hannibal's elephants, Scipio arrayed his legions in long columns, like spears, pointing into the Carthaginian line. Light infantry placed sparsely between the columns could choose either to attack the elephants or allow them to pass harmlessly to the rear. The use of elephants may seem ludicrous today, but one can easily imagine the fear they produced, thundering down on men

whose only defense was a shield and short sword; their influence on a battle was considerable unless tactics such as
Scipio devised were employed to stop them.

As the battle began, Hannibal ordered his majestic line
of elephants to charge. But suddenly the air was rent with a
blast of trumpets and horns! Every Roman trumpeter had
sounded his instrument at once. The unsteady beasts reared
in panic. Some plodded ponderously between the open lanes
of Roman infantry and into the wilderness. Others, struck by
a shower of darts and weighted javelins, turned about in
pain and became tangled among the Punic cavalry. Masinissa
charged viciously, putting the Carthaginian horsemen to
flight. He pursued them over the horizon—indeed so far that
Scipio feared Masinissa would not return in time to play his
most important role.

Meanwhile, the first two lines of Hannibal's infantry
broke under the weight of the Roman advance. Balaeric
slingers, Mauretanian archers, Gallic and Ligurian troops—
all fell back toward Carthage's last line of defense, the
veterans of Cannae. Well rested, more numerous than their
weary and bloodied opponents, Hannibal's invincible soldiers
waited—their spears lowered for action. They were a reserve
force prepared "to speak the last word" in the battle.

After a pause for water, Scipio moved two units to the
flanks, hoping to envelop Hannibal. But the experienced
African leader had anticipated the move. He countered by
extending his line as rapidly as Scipio had. The Roman
forces were in serious trouble.

Just then Scipio caught in his field of vision what must
have been a thrilling sight. Masinissa had returned! He
swooped down at full tilt upon the rear ranks of Hannibal's
veterans. It was Cannae all over again, but with a different
victim inside the circle of iron.

Most of the Punic soldiers died fighting where they
stood; few escaped the encirclement. The slaughter continued well into the afternoon when—too late—western

Numidian horsemen led by the sons of Syphax charged onto the scene. Had they arrived earlier, the result of Zama might have been vastly different. Scipio must have known that, too, when he chose the moment to launch his attack.

Hannibal was one of the survivors. On reaching his camp at Hadrumentum, he sent word to the Shofets of Carthage: "We have lost not only a battle but the war. Accept the terms of peace offered you."

Scipio had no desire for an extended siege at the walls of Carthage. He demanded almost the same terms as in the peace of 203 which Carthage had broken:

—Spain, Corsica, and Sardinia were to be ceded to Rome;
—Roman fugitives and deserters were to be returned;
—Punic warships, all but ten, and all the elephants were to be surrendered;
—Masinissa was to be given as a gift all African land "held by him or his forefathers";
—Carthage was to pay an indemnity of 10,000 talents in silver over fifty years;
—Carthage was to agree not to enter upon a future war in Africa without the consent of Rome;
—Carthage was to become the "friend and ally of the Roman Republic" (by this phrase Carthage became a tributary and vassal state of Rome).

Despite the severity of these terms Carthage was permitted to remain free. It was still in possession of its African territory. Its wealth and commerce were intact; so was its government. The future was not altogether hopeless.

Hannibal realized this. But in debating the treaty, some members of the Carthaginian Council did not. They called for a renewal of the war. Hannibal strode to the rostrum. He roughly dragged down from the lectern a speaker loudly demanding the recruitment of a new army and navy. A murmur of protest ran through the crowd.

"Forgive me," said Hannibal disarmingly. "Having left

you as a boy of nine, I return now after thirty-six years. I know something of the encampment and its ways, but you will have to instruct me in the customs of the city and this assembly."

Hannibal virtually shamed the Council into ratifying the treaty. He asked the members what terms they would have imposed on Rome had the situation been reversed. Were they not grateful that they and not a Roman proconsul were in authority? Would further war gain them better terms—or worse? Hannibal's view prevailed. The treaty was adopted.

Scipio returned to the Italian peninsula as a conquering hero. His progress toward Rome was marked from town to town with wild rejoicing. He was honored as *princeps senatus* (First Senator) and as *Africanus*. Yet in the privacy of the Senate chambers he, too, found some who cried for a renewal of the war. They grumbled at his generosity to Carthage and asked why the Punic city had not been destroyed. But the public adulation for Scipio was too great, and as in Carthage, the treaty was adopted.

Peace was achieved, therefore, only by the personal influence of two great warriors: Hannibal and Scipio. Some, such as the great German historian, Mommsen, long have speculated on why that should be. Is it possible that in their confrontation on the plain of Zama (or in a secret meeting later) the two reached some kind of understanding? Was it their aim to bring the war to an end, holding both victor and vanquished within reasonable bounds of sanity? Nobody, of course, will ever know. In the years that followed Zama, however, we can trace an unusual sympathy between the two extraordinary commanders of the Second Punic War.

With the end of the war Hannibal was, for the first time in his adult life, not in command of an army. What would he do?

# CHAPTER 9

# AFTER ZAMA

Life in retirement seldom pleases men such as Hannibal. After staring death in the face almost daily for seventeen years, fording icy streams, sleeping under the stars, making decisions that affected the fate of empires, he could hardly be expected to settle willingly for the placid life of the city bureaucrat. Nor would the people of Carthage allow him to. They still thought of him as their commander, idolized him for his triumphs. He was their hope for the future.

Hannibal was an aristocrat—wealthy, landed. But in Italy the lower classes in the towns had sided with him, seen him as a liberator from upper-class oppression. It was the same in Carthage. Although the members of his own class did not dare oppose him openly, many were jealous of his popularity. They feared that he would use his political power against the interests of the rich.

In 201 B.C. Scipio evacuated the last of his legions from Carthage. This was in accord with the treaty and his personal pledge to Hannibal. Even though the Roman troops were gone, the city still faced a monumental crisis—payment of the first year's indemnity to the conquerors. No longer could Carthage depend on silver from the mines of Spain. With much reluctance it was decided to impose a tax on personal wealth. Never before had the rich been asked to contribute from their own pockets, not even when Hannibal's army of

Italy was in desperate straits. Some of the Council's aristocrats, in their shame and hurt pride, wept openly. It is told that on seeing this, Hannibal laughed bitterly.

The leader of the aristocrats, known as "Kid" Hasdrubal, upbraided the general for laughing at the miseries which he himself had brought on them. Hannibal responded that he did not laugh at their weeping: "I laugh to see you weeping over the least of your misfortunes. You should have wept when our arms were taken from us and our fleet destroyed, when we were forbidden even to defend ourselves. Now you shed tears at the loss of a part of your private wealth."

Hannibal shed no tears. He was elected Shofet by popular vote; in reality he was the virtual dictator of Carthage. In peace as in war, he applied his total energies to a job. Working night and day, he reversed the decline of the Carthaginian state and began to restore it to a position of power in the Mediterranean.

He strengthened the tiny Punic army permitted by the peace treaty. He then sent the soldiers to escort commercial caravans probing the African interior for new trade contacts. He arranged for the irrigation of arid lands, turning them into profitable farms for his veterans. He reforested burned-over districts. He reformed the government, eliminating the lifetime tenure of the city's governing board. Henceforth the members of this board would be chosen by the people in an annual election. Finally, in a feat of astonishing skill, he put Carthage's finances on a sound basis. This he accomplished by ending the rampant thievery of a great flock of tax collectors who milked the poor and kept them poor. Every citizen was now held responsible for his fair share of taxation.

Hannibal transformed the Carthaginian state so well that it soon regained its place as the commercial capital of the western Mediterranean. In 191 B.C., eleven years after the disaster of Zama, Carthage was able to present in one shipment of solid silver bars the remaining installments of its indemnity to Rome—forty years in advance! It was an accomplishment every bit as remarkable as Hannibal's victories on the battlefield.

Hannibal was no longer in Carthage when the final payment was forwarded to Rome. In strengthening the state, he made powerful enemies. A party of Carthaginian nobles sailed to Rome in 195 B.C. to complain that their dictator was secretly preparing an army in violation of the treaty. Their tales met ready acceptance on the Capitoline Hill. Roman visitors to the Punic city already had returned with stories of Carthage's fantastic wealth—palaces gleaming with alabaster and silver, perfumed public baths, women adorned in costly jewels.

At the same time, the victorious Romans had been constantly at war. Ligurian and Gallic tribesmen remained unsubdued; rebellion flared in Spain despite ruthless measures taken by Roman occupation armies; in the east Rome was again at war with Philip V of Macedon.

It was easy enough for the Roman Senators to blame an unrepentant Carthage for Rome's colonial problems growing out of the Punic Wars. And it was easier still to believe the whining African envoys and focus all of Rome's frustration on the hated name of Hannibal.

Accordingly, a committee of the Senate was dispatched to bring charges of conspiracy against the Punic commander. Scipio Africanus protested strongly. Such interference in the affairs of another state, he said, was "unworthy" of Rome. He was overruled.

When the inquisitors came to claim him, Hannibal was gone. On the day the Romans docked in the city's still magnificent harbor, he showed himself conspicuously in the streets and public buildings. That evening he mounted a horse readied for him at the city gate, telling his servants to wait for him there. Alone and without baggage he galloped off into the night—not for a cooling ride across the moonlit countryside but for a 130-mile dash along the coast to his

villa near Hadrumentum. There he boarded a ship loaded for
him with silver bullion and set sail for the east.

Just one day later Hannibal put in at the tiny
Phoenician port of Cercina. He was recognized at once; and
although the reception for him was warm, speed and secrecy
were what he needed.

Improvising as only Hannibal could, he invited the sea
captains of the town to feast with him on shore, suggesting
they bring their heavy canvas sails to serve as awnings
against the sun. They agreed. Fueled by immense quantities
of Greek wine, the party lasted through the night. By the
time the Phoenician captains awoke from their stupor the
next morning and re-rigged their sails, Hannibal was far out
to sea, his destination and route still a secret.

He landed at Tyre, the Phoenician mother city, and was
received with honor and reverence. From there he went on to
Antioch and then to the royal court at Ephesus. This was his
real goal. At Ephesus he was warmly embraced by Antiochus
the Great of Syria—next to Hannibal Rome's most bitter
enemy. The Romans had succeeded in bringing together two
men who might never have joined forces against them.

Meanwhile, in Carthage, the aristocrats who had betrayed Hannibal confiscated his property and declared him
an outlaw. To placate the Roman envoys, who were infuriated by his escape, they burned the Barca palace to the
ground.

Hannibal's years with Antiochus proved stormy and un-
rewarding. The Carthaginian genius was at his best when in
sole command. True, he had planned campaigns with Hanno
and Carthalo, or with his brothers, poring intently over every
detail of an action so that nothing would be left to chance,
but dealing with an eastern monarch and his lackeys was
something different. In the court of Antiochus planning took
place in a formal War Council, and there the Carthaginian's

views usually did not prevail. Great diplomat though he was, Hannibal could not conceal his exasperation with the vain, arrogant Antiochus—always overconfident of himself and his armies. The Syrian leader consistently deluded himself, substituting high-flown rhetoric for military might. Nor would Hannibal stoop to deception and flattery—the language of the Syrian court—to gain his ends.

Antiochus considered himself the successor to Alexander the Great. The people of the east, at his royal orders, worshipped him. But the Romans, only barbarians in his mind, treated him with thinly disguised contempt. Antiochus already possessed the greater part of the former empire of Alexander the Great and was eager to regain the rest, including Greece. This, however, would certainly result in war with Rome, since the Romans considered themselves the protectors of the Greeks.

Hannibal argued strenuously against a major war with Rome before a powerful fleet could be built and an army trained for battle. A grand alliance might be formed; the manpower of Carthage and Spain and Gaul could be enlisted. Then the target would be Italy itself.

Others, men of less-sweeping vision, disagreed. It was they who had the ear of the King. They persuaded him that he would be welcomed in Greece as a liberator, that the Greeks would flock to his side against their Roman "protectors."

Mounting an expedition of slightly more than 10,000 men, Antiochus sent his generals across the Aegean to do battle with the Roman empire. To his surprise, only a handful of Aetolians joined him. At the historic pass of Thermopylae the Roman legions cut his little force to shreds. Only Antiochus and some 500 others lived to see Ephesus again.

More willing to listen to Hannibal after his return, Antiochus fitted out a fleet. But it was too late. With Hannibal commanding in his last battle—his very first one at sea—the Syrian galleys were unable to break the blockade of Ephesus.

Several months later Antiochus abandoned the Dardanelles and Roman soldiers crossed into Asia. In 190 B.C. a Roman force commanded by Publius Cornelius Scipio Africanus destroyed the Syrian army in a decisive engagement at Magnesia.

The war was over. Rome had won. By the terms of peace Hannibal was to be surrendered. But when Roman agents came for him, they discovered that, once again, the elusive Carthaginian had escaped their grasp.

For a time Hannibal took refuge on the island of Crete. Legend has it that he played a clever trick on the Cretans. Knowing the island to be infested by pirates, he ostentatiously deposited with the priests of the temple there a number of great vases for safe keeping. Although they were actually filled with lead, Hannibal carefully sprinkled the top of the vases with a layer of gold and silver coins. He concealed his real treasure in a number of hollow bronze idols which he left scattered near the entrance to his house. The old statues aroused no suspicion.

Eventually, as the Punic leader must have expected, Roman spies tracked him down. With capture imminent, he fled the island—calmly gathering up his bronze idols at the very last moment. One can only speculate on the reaction of the greedy Cretans when they rushed to the temple and smashed open the vases of "silver and gold."

For the next few years Hannibal lived quietly as the guest of Prusias, King of Bithynia. Yet even there, in that remote Black Sea kingdom, the Romans hounded him. When the Bithynians quarreled with an ally of Rome they were required to send a delegation to the city on the Tiber. One of their envoys let the carefully guarded secret slip—Hannibal was in Bithynia!

The Senate immediately authorized a small expedition to seize the great Carthaginian. Like a specter he had risen to haunt them in all their campaigns, from the Pillars of Hercules (where he had organized the Spanish guerrillas) to the recent conquests in the east, beyond the Bosporus.

True to the barbarian code of hospitality, King Prusias refused to surrender his guest. But he prized his own welfare and safety over that of his friend, Hannibal. "If you want him," said Prusias, "you will have to take him yourselves." However, the King posted guards at all six entrances to Hannibal's large but simple house. Even the secret escape passage that Hannibal had prepared (with his usual foresight) was closed.

Seeing the guards, Hannibal realized that this, at last, was the moment which he had known would someday come. Taking a vial of poison he had long kept about him, he turned to his servants and called for a goblet of wine.

"Now," he said, "it is time to end the worry of the Romans, impatient as they are for the death of an old and hated man."

Drinking the poisoned wine, he died.

It was 183 B.C., the sixty-fourth year of his life.

In the same year, at the age of fifty-three, Scipio Africanus also died. The victor of Zama had remained quietly informed of Hannibal's whereabouts for many years. But always he kept his silence. In his later life Scipio's ambition deserted him. His single goal came to be the protection of the Greek city-states against exploitation, even that of his own country.

Scipio, too, died in exile, driven from Rome by the vindictive Cato, "the Censor." On the death of Cato's aged mentor, Quintus Fabius Maximus, Cato personally took up the task of punishing Hannibal. He never forgave Scipio for sparing Carthage when he could have destroyed it.

So it was that Hannibal and his conqueror both perished alone, far from their ungrateful cities.

# EPILOGUE

The Second Punic War has been described as the "World War" of ancient times. Conflict raged from the Pillars of Hercules to the Balkan peninsula. Both sides fought with a fearful intensity and doggedness. Carthage lost, but Italy was ravaged—some 400 towns destroyed, hundreds of thousands killed. In southern Italy, occupied by Hannibal for fifteen years, most of the land was laid waste; even today the region remains impoverished.

As homeless agricultural workers poured into the cities for protection, the character of Roman life was suddenly and violently transformed. Trade began to prosper; manners and morals changed; idle masses of city dwellers demanded a role in politics. Meanwhile, the influx of precious metals from Spain enabled Romans to cultivate a taste for refinements and luxuries. This, in turn, encouraged still further conquests and the extortion of money and grain from the provinces.

Rome ceased to be a rude peasant civilization proud of its Spartan toughness. It absorbed some of the very corruptions it despised.

The form of government suitable for a small republic ceased to serve the purposes of a world empire. The constitution was weakened to permit talented or popular commanders like Scipio to remain in the field beyond the legal time limits. In the century and a half following Zama the old republican institutions were eroded away until at last they collapsed. The axis of Roman history pivots on the Second Punic War. Rome was never again the same.

The war illustrates, too, it has been said, how a great man may be subdued by a great nation. All of Hannibal's wizardry, his incredible military genius and diplomatic skills, proved inadequate in the end. For they were outweighed by Rome's capacity for disciplined self-sacrifice, its sheer grit. Faced by the inexhaustible well of Italian manpower, Hannibal only succeeded in postponing the death of his city for another fifty years. Had he won at Zama, he probably would have lost somewhere else. Rome was too powerful, too insistent to be defeated, at least by a Carthaginian government more concerned with domestic comfort and commercial success than self-defense.

Still, it was Hannibal—not his opponents, Fabius or Scipio—who determined the course of events in the Mediterranean world for more than thirty years; Rome merely responded to the initiatives of the Carthaginian artist.

And artist he most certainly was in his own particular sphere—war. According to many, Hannibal stands alone, the greatest of soldiers. Without the impulsiveness of Napoleon, more thoughtful and inventive than Alexander, he is unequaled for overall planning ability and political forethought. He was the first to apply the guerrilla tactics of ambush, feint, and surprise to battles of massed armies. The Romans —like the French and the Americans in Vietnam—found themselves baffled by compact, swift-moving forces manipulated by a crafty intelligence. The difference is that Hannibal operated in a hostile land for a generation, thriving in spite of neglect by his unworthy home government. He was able to strike from hidden lairs—even from out of a mist, as at Trasimene—or to befuddle and destroy his enemy on an open plain without concealment, as at Cannae.

Many armies have adopted the mode of guerrilla warfare practiced by Hannibal. In the American Revolution irregular bands led by Sumter, Marion, and Pickens seriously hurt much larger, better-equipped British armies. During World War II the French "underground," Marshall Tito's partisans in Yugoslavia, and other Allied resistance forces continuously harassed the Nazis with similar methods. Ho Chi Minh and General Giap of North Vietnam and Fidel Castro and Che Guevara of Cuba also are heirs of Hannibal's tactics.

There is about Hannibal little of the flamboyance from which legends are spun. His life style was simple. He rarely ate more than one meal a day and lived in the outdoors. "Shade," he said, "is for women." He is connected in history with but one woman and that one his wife.

Hannibal was a master of self-control. He held his emotions under such tight rein that the times when he lost his temper have been woven into oft-repeated anecdotes. Like Scipio, he preferred the solitude of his thoughts, believing that a thinking man is least alone when he is by himself. Thus he kept his own counsel, made his own decisions.

The Romans accused him of cruelty. Certainly, Hannibal recognized, along with warriors of all times, the value of instilling fear in his enemies and the people of an occupied territory. Yet he never matched the horrors perpetrated by the Romans. What act of Hannibal's can compare with the callousness of the Consul Nero when, after his victory at the Metaurus, he cut off the head of Hasdrubal and cast it into the Carthaginian camp? Julius Caesar later executed 400,000 Gauls in a single day "to teach them obedience." As common practice Roman commanders cut off the hands of their prisoners. Hannibal, by contrast, scrupulously sought out the bodies of generals he defeated and gave them proper burial. Whenever he could, as after the battle of Zama, he tried to save lives by avoiding unnecessary conflict.

He had one passion—the preservation of his city. And during his lifetime that necessarily meant an undying struggle to halt the expansion of Rome. Often he reminded others of the oath he had sworn to his father as a nine-year-old boy, with one of his hands on the sacrificial lamb—the oath of eternal hostility to Rome. This was the task to which Hannibal consecrated his life.

If ever the great warrior's country merited such devotion, it was many years after his death—when Carthage itself was about to die.

The Romans never ceased to fear Carthage's revival. In the Senate, Marcus Portius Cato ("the Censor") urged in speech after speech that "Carthago delenda est!"—Carthage must be destroyed. Finally, the Senators agreed.

In 149 B.C. Rome officially declared war and launched an invasion.

In a frenzy of defiance the Carthaginians at last rose up to defend their city. Artisans stripped the public buildings for lead and iron to improvise weapons. Barricades were erected. Ships were constructed. Precious idols from the temple were melted down and made into swords. Women cut off their hair and fashioned it into rope for their husbands' bows and for the catapults.

For three years the gallant Carthaginians held out behind the massive fortifications of their ancient city.

Rome achieved its horrible purpose only when the Senate appointed a ferocious new commander. He was Publius Cornelius Scipio Aemilianus, a grandson by adoption of Scipio Africanus and related by blood to the Consul who had perished bravely at Cannae.

Scipio Aemilianus tightened the siege around Carthage, reducing the population almost to starvation. Then, by sheer power of his war machines, he breached the walls.

The heroic townspeople fought on from house to house, retreating finally to the highest point in the city, the hallowed Byrsa. Below them they lighted a colossal fire for a last defense.

Polybius, an eyewitness to the carnage, relates that with the situation completely hopeless, Hasdrubal, the leader of the Carthaginian resistance, came forward to ask a truce of Scipio Aemilianus.

Hearing a piercing shriek behind him, he turned to see his noble wife, her hair in wild disarray, her gown besmirched, raise her arm and point at him from the Byrsa.

"The coward groveling at the feet of that Roman is not my husband!" she cried. "He will be punished!"

With that, she gathered her young sons in her arms and flung them into the flames below, leaping after them to her death.

So perished Carthage—the legendary city of Dido.

The survivors of Carthage, numbering only 50,000 were sold into slavery, the city itself opened to plunder by the soldiers. Those citizens who escaped scattered into the Numidian and Libyan interior where they were lost to history forever.

Cato, on an inspection tour, ordered that all remaining buildings be leveled to the ground and put to the torch. The fire is said to have burned for seventeen days; a layer of rubble remains today. Then the land was plowed and sown with salt. Finally, before leaving the site, Scipio Aemilianus placed upon it his everlasting curse. He cursed all those who had ever occupied the city of Carthage, tilled its soil, fought in its armies. And he bequeathed a twofold curse on any who might return there or try to resurrect the ruins. "Let eternal silence and desolation remain here!" he said.

Little of Punic civilization has survived. Even when the city was at its height, its art was largely an imitation of objects imported from overseas. Commercial manuals flourished and were preserved by the practical Romans. Of the city's literature and intellectual life we know practically nothing. Primitive cruelty marred the Carthaginian religion, and stories of this were preserved by the Greeks and the Romans. What other aspects of the religion there may have been we can hardly surmise.

In dealing with the subject peoples of its empire, Carthage showed none of the willingness of Rome to share the benefits of citizenship. This meant that in the Punic Wars even the city's supposed allies might prove untrustworthy— as indeed was the case with the Numidians. With no stake of their own in the conflict, the Punic allies did not freely volunteer recruits and money as did the beleaguered cities of Latium and Campania. Nor was there in Carthage the germ of greatness that was to produce in Rome a high civilization and a bridge to modern times.

Indeed, if not for the remarkable achievements of Hannibal, Carthage would have but passing reference in the pages of history.

As it is, the ancient African city lives on, remembered always because of the achievements of its noblest leader.

# FOR FURTHER
# READING

It is to the eternal credit of Livy and Polybius that they accorded a full measure of honor in their histories to Rome's great adversary, Hannibal. Livy in particular should be the starting point for those interested in a detailed account of the Hannibalic War. Consult the Loeb Classical Library translation.

Secondary sources abound. Especially important is Theodore Mommsen's monumental five-volume *History of Rome*, which is vivid and colorful, but superseded in some points by more recent research. Thomas Arnold's *The Second Punic War*, although somewhat dated, is highly readable and essential for background detail. Among other older sources, biographies by Theodore Dodge and William O. Morris should prove especially rewarding to those interested in military strategy and tactics.

The contemporary study by Howard Scullard (*Scipio Africanus in the Second Punic War*) is vital for its scholarly insights. Of popular interest is Harold Lamb's *Hannibal: One Man Against Rome,* which is notable for its absorbing style and the provocative, if tenuous, thesis that Hannibal's struggle represented the final defense of Greek freedom against Roman imperial expansion. Leonard Cottrell's *Hannibal: Enemy of Rome* is also well-written, popularized history; the author attempts to follow personally every step of Hannibal's invasion route from Spain to Italy.

Finally, *The Road to Rome,* a quaintly lighthearted play by Robert Sherwood, projects onto the scene after Cannae a winsome but sexually frustrated Roman noblewoman whose intervention persuades Hannibal to spare the city.

# SOME
# IMPORTANT
# DATES

| | | |
|---|---|---|
| 218 | (November) | Battle of the Ticinus |
| 218 | (December) | Battle of the Trebia |
| 217 | (Spring) | Battle of Lake Trasimene. Q. Fabius Maximus made Dictator of Rome |
| 216 | (June) | Battle of Cannae (June by our reckoning; August by the Roman calendar) |
| 216 | | Capua joins Hannibal |
| 216–215 | | Winter quarters in Capua |
| 214 | | Syracuse joins Hannibal |
| 212 | | Syracuse recovered by Marcellus |
| 211 | | Hannibal's march to Rome |
| 211 | | Capua falls to Rome |
| 211 | | Defeat and death of the Scipios in Spain |
| 210 | | P. Cornelius Scipio (later Africanus) becomes Roman commander in Spain |
| 209 | | Scipio takes Cartagena |
| 207 | | Battle of the Metaurus. Hasdrubal defeated and killed by Nero |
| 206 | | Hannibal in Bruttium |
| 205 | | Scipio elected Consul; trains forces in Sicily |
| 205 | | Peace between Philip V of Macedon and Rome |
| 204 | (Spring) | Scipio invades Africa |
| 203 | | Death of Mago |
| 203 | | Hannibal returns to Africa |
| 202 | | Battle of Zama |
| 195 | | Flight of Hannibal to the east |
| 192–189 | | Roman war with Antiochus the Great and the Aetolians; Hannibal adviser to Antiochus |
| 190 | | Scipio Africanus defeats Antiochus at Magnesia |
| 183 | | Death of Scipio Africanus |
| 183 | | Death of Hannibal in Bithynia |
| 149–146 | | Third Punic War, ending in total destruction of Carthage |

# INDEX

74 0865                              c 1

jB          Jacobs, William Jay
HANNI
BAL         Hannibal, an
               African hero

| DATE | | | |
|---|---|---|---|
| MAR 1 0 1975 | | | |
| JUL 1 6 1975 | | | |
| OCT 1 4 1975 | | | |
| | | | |
| | | | |
| | | | |
| | | | |
| | | | |
| | | | |
| | | | |
| | | | |